THE MITCHELL BEAZLEY POCKET GUIDE TO

Trees

Keith Rushforth

Nomenclature

Popular names of trees vary widely; this makes them unreliable, and accuracy is best served by employing the scientific (Latin) name, the structure of which is governed by strict international rules. All trees have a double name: the first element is that of the genus, and the second the name of the species within the genus. For example, the birches are known as the *Betula* genus, and the Silver birch is the pendula species, and so the Silver birch is known as *Betula pendula*. Genera with noticeable similarities are grouped into families, and *Betula* belongs in the Betulaceae.

Sometimes further definition is required beyond the species. A variety (indicated by "var." after the specific name or subspecies ("ssp.") is a tree that has developed slightly different characteristics from its species (or "type") due to regional ecological factors. A cultivar or clone is propagated vegetatively from a cutting from a tree that showed some minor genetic change. It is given a new name, which is printed in inverted commas. A hybrid (denoted by "x" between the genetic and specific names) is a natural cross between two species. Where the parentage of a hybrid is in doubt, as with many Prunus hybrids, a popular name replaces the specific name and the trees are listed as cultivars with the names in single quotes.

Acknowledgements

The author and publishers would like to thank the following people and organizations for their help:
Alf Westall and Malcolm Scott, Bedgebury National Pinetum, Kent; **Alan Mitchell**, The Forestry Commission, Alice Holt Lodge, Farnham, Surrey; **Jim Keesing and Charles Erskine**, The Royal Botanic Gardens, Kew; **Ivan Hicks**, West Dean Estates, Chichester, Sussex.

Artwork

Jacket: **John Michael Davis**
Francesca Ross: 6, 20, 106/107 **Olivia Beasley**: 22/23, 28/29, 32/49, 52/59; **John Davis**: 73/83, 130/145; **John Michael Davis**: 21, 26/27, 30/31, 50/51, 60/69, 116/129, 146/167; **Annabel Milne and Peter Stebbing**: 5/8, 11/20, 24/25, 70/72, 168/188; **David Moore**: 1, 84/97, 106/115; **Paul Wrigley**: 98/105

Edited and designed by
Mitchell Beazley Publishers Limited
part of Reed International Books Ltd,
Michelin House, 81 Fulham Road, London SW3 6RB
© Mitchell Beazley Publishers 1980
Reprinted 1981, 1982, 1983, 1984, 1986, 1988, 1990, 1991, 1992
Revised Edition 1996
ISBN 1 85732 7713
Colour reproduction by Photoprint Plates Ltd
Produced by Mandarin Offset
Printed in Malaysia

Contents

Introduction

This book is a field guide that will enable the reader to identify almost any tree he or she encounters. Although Great Britain boasts only some 35 native species, many other introduced species are familiar. In this book we have been able to illustrate over 350 species as well as mention other species, varieties and cultivars. This means that all commonly encountered trees, with the exception of those rarely found outside arboreta, should be readily identifiable.

There is a generally accepted order in which tree families should be placed, based upon their presumed evolutionary sequence from the more primitive to the advanced groups. Occasionally I have deviated from this in order to place side by side species which bear a strong resemblance to each other so that they may be more readily identified. Within families the genera have been ordered purely for the sake of convenience, and their sequence does not imply any botanical significance.

A tree is usually defined as a woody perennial plant growing on a single stem to a height of 6 m or more, whereas a shrub does not attain this height and has a stem divided near the ground. But of course plants do not fall obligingly into these man-made categories all the time, and some of them occur as either a tree or a shrub. The rule I have followed is that if a plant occurs as a tree with more than a negligible frequency, then it should be included. Two plants included on these grounds, but often excluded from tree books, are Juniper and Ivy. I have also tried to pay particular attention to the appearance of deciduous trees in winter, a phase of their existence all too often ignored in books.

Points about size can only be made in general terms; this particularly concerns the bole or trunk, which increases in diameter every year – a distinctive characteristic of the growth of trees. The girth of the trunk 1.5 m above the ground is a reasonable method of estimating the age of a tree, and the rate of growth shows a remarkable degree of consistency amongst the species. The average increase in girth of a tree growing in the open is 2.5 cm a year; thus, if it has a girth of about 2.5 m, it is about 100 years old. The celebrated yew slows down after 100 years, and with a girth of 10 m could be up to 1,000 years old. All measurements given in the book are maxima.

How to use this book

The annotated illustrations, text and symbols, which are explained below, give in concise form all the information necessary to identify a tree, but you do not need to thumb your way laboriously through the book looking for the right species. The first step is to read the introductory pages, where the major differences between groups of trees are explained, and guidance is given on which parts of the tree to examine to narrow the choice. Once in the field you can use the three keys to identify the genus; from there you can proceed quickly to the species in question. Before you try to identify an unknown tree it is a good idea to practise using the keys by working backwards from one that is familiar.

More general matter will be found in the introduction to the broadleaf trees, p70.

Symbols

R	Rare, usually found only in collections	🌱	Needles in fascicles of 5
🌳	Deciduous, i.e. leaves shed in autumn	🌿	Leaves in horizontal sprays along shoot
🌲	Evergreen, leaves retained into winter	🌳	Found in deciduous woods
🍃	Buds and leaves alternate or spiral	🌲	Found in evergreen woods
🍃	Buds and leaves in opposite pairs	🌳	Found in mixed woods
🌿	Leaves awl- or scale-like	🏠	Common in streets, parks and gardens
🌾	Leaves in rosettes on short (spur) shoots	🌳	Found in open countryside
V	Needles in fascicles of 2	💧	Found by water or on wet or moist sites
Ⅶ	Needles in fascicles of 3	♂ male ♀ female	

Abbreviations

alt	alternate	lf	leaf			sim	similar
br	branch	lflt	leaflet			sp(p)	species
c.	about	lvs	leaves				(plural)
cm	centimetre	m	metre			uns	underside
cv	cultivar	mm	millimetre			ups	upperside
fl	flower	opp	opposite			var	variety
fr	fruit	sev	several			vn	vein
infl	inflorescence	sh	shoot			yr	year

How to identify trees

The identification of trees is a matter of putting together all the various pieces of information provided by the plant, not just relying on some of them. It is very tempting to latch on to some immediately striking feature and go no further, in which case you might well end up wrongly identifying a tree, as your only piece of evidence was misleading. For instance, you might know that ashes are generally characterized by pinnate leaves, and so never entertain the possibility that the tree in front of you with single leaves is an ash – but there is an exception to the rule, the Single-leafed cultivar of ash which is often found in older parks or gardens. So whenever possible examine the foliage, buds, flowers, fruit, habit and bark, or as many as are visible at that time of the year.

The first step, before using the keys in this book, is to decide whether a tree belongs to the conifers or the broadleaf trees, something almost anybody can do. The actual difference is that the conifers have exposed ovules (which develop into seeds) whereas the broadleaf trees bear theirs enclosed in an ovary, but for identification purposes the differences indicated by the colloquial names of the groups are sufficient: the conifers bear cones, and have needle-like leaves which contrast with the wider foliage of the broadleaf trees.

Besides observing as many features as possible, bear in mind a few general points. Even within the plant, leaf character varies, the leaves at the top generally being smaller (although poplars are a notable exception). The number of lobes usually decreases with age, and a fine example of this is Holly. Remember that shoots of a tree that has been pruned will grow with abnormal vigour, giving rise to untypical proportions. As a rule you will find more typical features on short shoots. Features which generally occur in pairs can be found in threes or even fours, for example sycamore fruits and the buds of Raywood ash.

Foliage characteristics

Foliage should be examined thoroughly. First, important observations can be made at some distance from the tree itself, such as the colour of the foliage, and whether or not it is pendent (hanging). With more detailed examination, leaves provide clues in variation of outline, and the way they are set upon the shoot. Other features to look at are the margins, the shape of the base and tip, the veins and the petiole, and the texture and hairiness.

Conifers: the illustrations below show four types of leaf arrangement. **Fascicles** (a), borne by pines, are bunches of needles growing from one bud (needle is not a scientific term but simply a descriptive alternative to leaf). Leaves set in a **pectinate row** (b), such as those of the yews and firs, are arranged in ranks along opposite sides of the shoot. **Awl-shaped leaves** (c), as borne by the junipers, are set radially around the shoot, in whorls or pairs. **Scale-like leaves** (d), set densely round the shoot, are characteristic of Lawson cypress. See also p19.

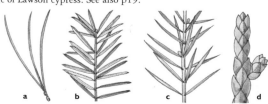

a   b   c   d

Broadleaf trees: the illustrations below show some basic leaf shapes of broadleaf trees, which have more varied foliage than the conifers. An important point to remember is that these are mostly deciduous, and are found in their mature form for a relatively short time.

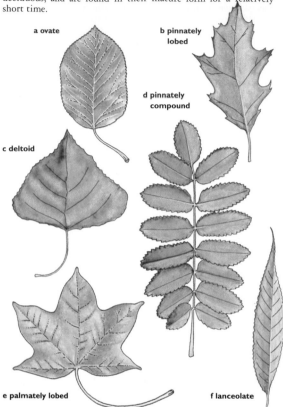

a ovate

b pinnately lobed

d pinnately compound

c deltoid

e palmately lobed

f lanceolate

Besides the basic shape, look at the **margins** (the edges of the leaf), which are serrated in **a, c, d & f** and entire in **b**; the **apex** (the end of the leaf farthest from the shoot), which is acute (or pointed) in **c** and acuminate (or drawn out) in **a**; and the **base** of the leaf, which is rounded in **a**, cuneate (or wedge-shaped) in **b** and **f**, truncate (or squared) in **c** and cordate (or heart-shaped) in **e**. See also the introduction to broadleaf trees, p70.

a

b

c

The **petiole** or leaf stalk (above) can provide useful clues when its shape, particularly in cross-section, is examined. It is usually round **a** but can also be grooved **b**, as in Wild cherry, or flattened **c**, as in Aspen. There is a bud at the base of the petiole, and usually the petiole is curved around it in a crescent shape. In some species, however, the bud is completely enclosed in the enlarged petiole base during the growing season; when the leaf falls, it leaves a scar which encircles the bud.

Shoots and buds

Shoots are the new growth that springs from the buds at the start of the new season. They usually harden into their mature wooden state by midsummer and are then ready to bear the buds for the next season's growth.

Points to look for on shoots are the colour, whether they are hairy or not, and their shape. Most shoots, when seen in cross-section, are round, but they can be angled or winged in some species. Cutting across a shoot reveals its basic structure, which is shown in illustration **c** below. In the centre there is always the **pith**, sometimes a useful identification guide; it is generally a soft amorphous mass of various colours and textures, but is occasionally chambered, as in **b**.

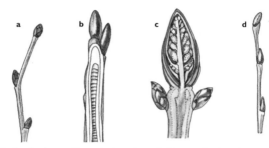

The **buds**, borne through the winter before producing the new growth, are a key identification feature. There is usually a single bud on the end of the shoot, known as the terminal bud, from which the shoot will continue to grow. Lateral buds are arranged along the sides of the shoot, and produce new lateral shoots or leaves. The way in which these lateral shoots are arranged can vary considerably, and the main differences are illustrated above – set alternately as in **a**, **b** and **d**, or in opposite pairs as in **c**.

Buds are a useful identification guide where they are set in different ways; a few trees, such as the cypresses, do not have a terminal bud in winter, while oaks are distinctive, having a cluster of buds at the shoot tips. Many trees have buds laid down and covered by the bark; they remain dormant until the main shoot is damaged or more light reaches the bole, when they start growing and produce epicormic shoots. These shoots usually have larger, softer and hairier leaves but are often all that can be reached.

Other features to look for in buds are the shape, size and colour. Buds may be ovoid, round, conic, cylindrical or spindle-shaped. Some species may have resinous or sticky buds **c**. One other key feature is the number of scales on the outside of each bud: some may be naked and have no scales at all, or they may have one **d**, two **b** or many scales **a** and **c**, usually adpressed on top of each other.

Thorns

Thorns are characteristic of a few species and occasional in others. The first and most obvious difference is the number in which they occur: the illustrations above show typical formations of thorns which grow in ones **a**, twos **b** or threes **c**. They are usually derived from shoots, and often carry buds at the base **a**.

Bark

The bark, the protective outer covering of the stem, can be a useful identification feature. Although the young branches have smooth bark, that on the bole is usually split and broken as the diameter of the stem increases with age. It is the form that this breaking takes which can be diagnostic, and the chief characteristics, such as colour, are usually more pronounced in the bark higher up in the tree than in the mature bark near the base, usually because it has fissured or flaked more recently. Three basic types of bark are shown in the illustrations below: scaly fissures **a**, peeling bark **b** and ridged and furrowed bark **c**. The fissure colour can be important.

a b c

Glossary

Adpressed Closely pressed to an adjoining part of the plant, such as a bud against a twig or shoot (Hornbeam p93)
Alternate Leaves arranged singly along and on both sides of a stem, usually helically
Aril Fleshy outer covering of a seed (Yew p22)
Auricles Ear-like appendages at the base of a leaf (Pedunculate oak p99)
Awl-like leaves Small leaves tapering to a slender, sharp point (Juniper p34)
Axil Upper angle formed between a twig and a shoot, or the junction between two veins
Axil tufts Pubescence in axil

Bipinnate Advanced type of pinnate leaf whose leaflets are themselves pinnate (Honey locust p146)
Blade Greatest part of a leaf, the part other than the leaf stalk
Bloom Powdery or waxy sheen of a shoot or leaf (Eucalyptus p113) which can easily be rubbed away
Bole Trunk or stem of a tree
Bract Modified leaf associated with a flower. In some trees they are more conspicuous than the flowers themselves (Dove tree p173); in conifers bract scales often extend beyond the edge of the fertile scales (p19)
Buttress Strengthened part of a bole or root that assists in supporting a tree (Beech p94)

Calyx Green cup of sepals, outside the petals, supporting the flower
Carpel Single unit of a flower comprising the stigma, style and ovary
Catkin Dense, usually long and pendent, group of flowers (Hazel p92)
Chambered pith Pith of a shoot that is broken up by hollow spaces (Walnut p84)
Ciliate Leaves having a hairy fringe to their margins
Columnar-conic Shape of a habit which is narrow and straight sided at its base and then becomes pyramidal
Compound Leaves comprising several separate leaflets
Coppicing The practice of cutting back trees such as willows to their stumps in order to promote growth
Cordate Heart-shaped; used especially of leaves (Mulberry p113) where the leaf bases curve away from the leaf stalk
Corymb Domed or flat-topped flower cluster with the external flowers opening first (p71)
Crenate Serration which has broad, rounded teeth
Crown Upper part of the tree; the branches and foliage
Cultivar Variety of tree selected in cultivation

Cuneate Wedge-shaped base of a leaf tapering into leaf stalk (Cork oak p102)
Cupule Circle of bracts which become cup-shaped and enclose fruit such as an acorn
Cyme Flat-topped flower cluster, the central flowers opening first

Dioecious Having male and female flowers on separate trees
Drupe Fruit containing a seed in the form of a stone

Entire Margin without either teeth or lobules
Exserted Extended beyond the surrounding component

Fascicle Bundle or cluster (p6)
Fastigiate Tree habit which has very upswept, almost erect branches (Lombardy poplar p75, Cypress oak p99)
Fluted With alternate ridges and grooves (Dawn redwood p38)

Glabrous Smooth
Glaucous Covered with a blue-grey or whitish bloom
Globose Irregularly spherical

Habit General appearance of a tree, usually from a distance
Hilum Paler, basal seed scar of a nut (Yellow buckeye p167)
Hybrid Species arising from the cross fertilization of two specifies with the names separated by an "x" (*Tilia* x *euchlora*)

Imbricate Overlapping like roof tiles
Impressed vein Vein set below surface of leaf (Hornbeam p93)
Inflorescence Floral part of a plant
Involucre Circle of bracts developed to cover a fruit (Beech p94)

Lanceolate Shaped like the blade of a spear, as most willow leaves (Crack willow p80)
Layering The ability of a tree to regenerate by a branch touching the ground where it roots and forms a new plant
Leader Leading shoot of tree

and so one of the youngest; may droop and thereby be an identification feature (Western hemlock p58)
Leaf scar Imprint left on a twig or shoot of a fallen leaf. Also known as "leaf trace"
Lenticel Raised corky breathing pore on twig or shoot
Lobe Rounded or angular side projection on a leaf
Lobulate Bearing small lobes

Margin Leaf edge
Midrib Central vein of a leaf
Monoecious Having both male and female flowers on the same tree although the male and female flowers may be separate (eg. Hazel p92)

Oblique Unequal-sided base of a leaf, as in most elms (p108)
Obovate Ovate with the widest part beyond the middle of the leaf
Obovoid Ovoid and largest beyond the middle
Operculum Cap of fused petals that covers flower bud of Eucalyptus (p174), falls as flower opens
Opposite Set in pairs at the same level each side of the twig or shoot
Orbicular Almost circular-shaped leaf
Ovate Leaf that is egg-shaped in outline, widest below the middle (p6)
Ovule Part of the plant that becomes the seed after fertilization

Palmate Leaf that has lobes or leaflets radiating from one simple point, like the fingers of a hand (p6)
Panicle Compound inflorescence whose flowers branch from a central stem
Pectinate 2-ranked arrangement of leaves either side of a central shoot in the nature of the teeth of a comb
Peduncle Flower stalk
Peltate Shield-shaped
Perfect Having male and female organs combined in one flower and not as separate flowers (Crab apples p130)

Petiole Leaf stalk
Petiolule The stalk attaching leaflets to a rachis
Pinna Leaflet or primary division of a pinnate leaf
Pinnate Compound leaf with leaflets arranged regularly each side of a rachis (p6)
Pith Softer, central section of a shoot's stem
Pollarding The practice of lopping trees at about 3 m or more above the ground in order to encourage further growth
Pome Fruit of several carpels enclosed in thick flesh (Crab apple p130)
Pubescence Covering of soft and short hairs
Pulvinus Swelling on some conifer shoots from which each leaf grows (p40)

Raceme Inflorescence of stalked flowers growing from a rachis
Rachis Central stalk of a compound (pinnate) leaf or inflorescence

Samara Winged fruit (Sycamore p155)
Serrate Toothed
Sessile Non-stalked

Sheath Tubular envelope enclosing a bunch of fascicle leaves (Pine p40)
Simple Leaf consisting of one single blade (Tulip tree p119)
Sinuate Strongly waved
Sinus Recess between lobes
Stipule Appendage usually at the base of a petiole
Stomata Orifices in a leaf used to let air into the leaf
Sub-sessile With a minute stalk

Ternate Set in threes
Tomentose Having a dense, woolly pubescence
Trifoliate Leaf comprising 3 leaflets
Truncate Abrupt end to a leaf base or tip

Umbel Inflorescence with pedicels all arising from the same point (p71)
Umbo Raised centre of the scale of a pine cone

Valve Section into which a fruit capsule splits
Venation Pattern of veins
Vein Rib of a leaf
Vein axils Upper angle between two veins

Identification keys

Don't shy away from botanical keys; they are a tried and tested aid to tree identification. The keys to conifers, broadleaf trees and leafless winter shoots included here will lead you to the genus of the tree concerned; from the page numbers given you can quickly locate the species in question.

To use these keys, select a good specimen and progress through the listed options the key offers. If the answer to the first part of a choice is "yes", move on to the name or number indicated; if "no" when only one choice is offered, move to the next number. Eventually you will reach the genus (or selection of genera) to which your species belongs. In winter, there is nothing to prevent you using the broadleaf key on fallen or dried leaves or using the leafless shoot key while the shoots are still leafy.

Learn to use the keys with a species already familiar to you. With practice you will find that their use, together with detailed observation in the field, will greatly improve your knowledge of trees and your ability to identify them.

Preliminary key

1   **a** Tree in leaf   2
    b Tree not in leaf   **Key C**

2   **a** Leaf needle – or scale-like; veins
    absent or (more rarely) parallel   **Key A**
    b Main veins branched, reticular   **Key B**
    c Leaf veins parallel, leaves more
    than 30 cm *Cordyline* 188 or
    Trachycarpus 188

Key A Conifer trees

1   **a** Lvs broad (over 4 mm), vns
    parallel   2
    b Lvs narrow or scale-like   3

2   **a** Lvs broadest at base, hard, sharp
    Araucaria 24
    b Lvs broadest at apex, soft, lobed,
    rounded *Gingko* 21

3   **a** Lvs set singly, in opp prs or
    whorls of 3   4
    b Lvs set spirally, singly or in
    bundles of 2–5   8

4   **a** Lvs linear, in fern-like fronds;
    new buds set below side shoots
    Metasequoia 38
    b Lvs scale- or awl-like   5

5   **a** Fruit berry-like; lvs set in 2s or 3s
    Junipers 34
    b Fr a cone, lvs always paired   6

6   **a** Foliage in flat sprays   7
    b Foliage in 3-D sprays *Cupressus*
    25

7   **a** Cone rounded x *Cupressocyparis*
    27 or *Chamaecyparis* 28
    b Cone flask-shaped *Thuja*/*Biota*
    32, *Thujopsis* 33 or *Calocedrus* 34

8   Lvs long (10–15 cm), in spaced
    whorls *Sciadopitys* 39

9   **a** Lvs thin-textured, set in fern-like
    fronds *Taxodium* 37
    b Lvs not as above   10

10   **a** Sh not green (except when very
    young)   11
    b Sh green or yellow-green for at
    least 2 yrs   16

11   Lvs in bundles of 2, 3 or 5 *Pinus* 60

12   **a** Lvs in rosettes on 2nd yr and
    older shs   13
    b Lvs always single, spaced along shs   14

13 a Lvs soft, turning yellow in autumn; cones have persistent, open scales *Larix* 52
  b Lvs hard; cones with deciduous scales *Cedrus* 50

14 Lvs set on prominent pegs projecting from shoot *Picea* 56 or (more rarely) *Tsuga* 58

15 a Cones small (under 3 cm), pendulous; buds very small (under 2 mm), rounded *Tsuga* 58
  b Cones over 3 cm, pendulous, persistent, with exserted, trident bracts; *Pseudotsuga* 49
  c Cones erect, over 5 cm, with deciduous scales *Abies* 41

16 a Lvs flat in x-section, parted on sh   17
  b Lvs round in x-section   19

17 Bark thick, very soft *Sequoia* 37

18 a Lvs spine-tipped, very sharp to touch *Torreya* 22
  b Lvs softer *Taxus* 22, *Podocarpus* 23 or *Saxegothaea* 23

19 a Lvs short (4–7 mm), pointed, dotted with stomata; bark thick, soft *Sequoiadendron* 36
  b Lvs longer (to 1.5 cm), less adpressed; bark thin, hard, stringy *Cryptomeria* 39

Key B Broadleaf trees
  • indicates that at least some species in the genus are evergreen

1 a Lvs in opp or nearly opp prs on sh   2
  b Lvs alt on sh   12
  c Lvs in whorls of 3, or both opp and alt *Lagerstroemia* 181, *Fraxinus* 182 (rarely) or *Catalpa* 187

2 a Lvs compound   3
  b Lvs simple   4

3 a Lvs pinnately compound *Euodia* 152, *Acer* 154, *Eucryphia*• 171 or *Fraxinus* 182
  b Lvs palmately compound *Acer* (rarely) 154 or *Aesculus* 166

4 a Lvs toothed or lobed   5
  b Lf margins entire (or with 1-2 prs of large teeth)   8

5 Lvs lobed or lobulate *Acer*• 154

6 Lvs thick, leathery, dark green
 Eucryphia• 171 or *Phillyrea*• 186

7 a Lvs narrowly oval; sh squarish
 Euonymus 152
 b Lvs ovate with cordate bases; sh
 rounded, brown *Cercidiphyllum* 115

8 a Lvs leathery, evergreen, glaucous
 or glossy above   9
 b Lvs not leathery, deciduous   11

9 a Lvs willow-like, felted white
 below *Olea*• 185
 b Lvs glabrous   10

10 a Lvs same both sides, glaucous
 Eucalyptus• 174
 b Lvs not same both surfaces, glossy
 above *Ligustrum*• 185

11 a Lvs less than 10 cm, veins curve
 parallel to margins *Cornus* 176
 b Lvs more than 10 cm *Paulownia*
 186 or *Catalpa* 187

12 a Lvs simple   20
 b Lvs pinnate   13
 c Lvs bipinnate *Gleditsia* 146,
 Acacia• 147 or *Koelreuteria* 171

13 Lvs always comprise 3 lflts
 Laburnum 148

14 Pith chambered, not solid *Juglans*
 84 or *Pterocarya* 85

15 Terminal lflt or 3 terminal lflts
 largest *Carya* 86

16 a Bud hidden in base of petiole   17
 b Bud not so hidden   18

17 a Sh rounded, smooth, green, yellow
 or paler *Gleditsia* 146, *Sophora* 147
 or *Rhus* 150
 b Sh ridged, brown *Robinia* 146

18 a Lflts entire or with 1–3 prs of teeth
 at base *Ailanthus* 149 or *Rhus* 150
 b Lflts toothed   19

19 a Toothing regular *Sorbus* 124 or
 Rhus 150
 b Toothing very coarse *Koelreuteria*
 171

20 Lvs have truncate bases, indented
 apexes *Liriodendron* 119

21 Lvs concentrated at sh tip, fewer
 along sh; fruit an acorn *Quercus* 98

22 Bk in upper crown smooth;
peeling orange and yellow-pink
Arbutus• 178

23 a Lf margins entire, toothless 24
b Lvs toothed or lobed 32

24 Lvs same both sides, pendulous
Eucalyptus• 174

25 Bk brown, flaking to yellow and
pink *Parrotia* 120

26 a Lf margins wavy or crinkled 27
b Lf margins flat 28

27 a Lvs very glossy, dark green above
Diospyros 179, *Laurus* 106
b Lvs pale green, slightly glossy
Pittosporum• 165
c Veins impressed, pubescent
below *Salix* 79

28 Lvs orbicular *Cercis* 145

29 Lvs have vns curving parallel to
margin *Cornus* 176

30 Lvs prominently 3-veined at or
near base *Celtis* 108, *Sassafras* 107

31 a Lvs elliptic to obovate *Salix*
79, *Magnolia•* 116, *Cotoneaster*
123 or *Nyssa* 172
b Lvs lanceolate *Embrothrium•* 119,
Cotoneaster• 125 or *Pyrus* 133
c Lvs elliptic to lanceolate, evergreen,
with a strong spicy odour when
crushed *Laurus* 106 or *Umbellularia* 107

32 a Lvs lobed 33
b Lvs toothed or lobulate, not lobed 37

33 a Vns arise at lf base (palmate vns) 34
b Vns arise along midrib (pinnate vns)
Crataegus 122 or *Sorbus* 124

34 Bud hidden in hollow base of petiole
Platanus 153

35 Lf uns densely hairy *Populus* 73

36 a Sinuses obtuse, rounded
Morus 113, *Ficus* 114 or
Kalopanax 175
b Sinuses acute *Liquidambar* 120 or
Kalopanax 175

37 Margins have spine-like teeth
Castanea 105 or *Ilex•* 151

38 Sh has bristly, glandular hrs *Corylus* 92

39 **a** Lvs rounded ovate, more than 4cm in
width, bases cordate or oblique
Tilia 168 or *Davidia* 173
b Lvs under 4cm wide, or not as above   40

40 Lvs deltoid or orbicular; petiole
flattened or lf uns "painted" white
Populus 73

41 **a** Pith finely chambered, fr
4-winged *Halesia* 181
b Pith solid   42

42 **a** Vns deeply impressed *Salix* 79,
Carpinus 93, *Nothofagus* 96 or
Parrotia 120
b Vns not deeply impressed   43

43 Petiole has 2 (1–4) glands near lf
blade *Prunus* 134

44 Lvs lanceolate *Salix* 79

45 Lf uns has silvery white pubescence
Sorbus 124 or *Malus* 130

46 Margins crinkled or wavy *Alnus* 90,
Fagus 94, *Stewartia* 172 or *Styrax*
180

47 Lvs obliquely based, doubly serrate *Ulmus*
107

48 Lvs oblong-obovate, 5–15 cm,
mostly stalkless, minutely toothed,
downy both sides *Mespilus* 123

49 Fruit a persistent, ovoid, woody
cone-like catkin *Alnus* 90

50 Fruit a cylindrical or ovoid catkin,
scales deciduous *Betula* 87

51 Lvs dark, shiny green, elliptic-oblong,
fruit strawberry-like *Arbutus•* 178

52 Teeth deep, single, in 12 or less prs
Zelkova 112 or *Ulmus* 107

53 Bark silvery-grey, fluted; lf vns parallel,
impressed *Carpinus* 93

54 Shoots have spines; fruit berry-like
Crataegus 122

55 **a** Flowers and fruits in umbels
Malus 130
b Flowers and fruits in racemes   55

56 Lvs nearly round or elliptic, densely
pubescent and glaucous below
Styrax 180

57 a Lvs under 5 cm, dull; fls in spring
       Amelanchier 121
    b Lvs over 5 cm, glossy; fls in autumn
       Oxydendrum 179

Key C Leafless winter shoots

1 a Buds in opp prs or whorls of 3   2
   b Buds alt along sh   11

2 Lf scars set above buds; bark
   fibrous, red-brown *Metasequoia* 38

3 a Buds with 2 outer scales   4
   b Buds with sev outer scales or none   5

4 a Buds elongated *Cornus* 176
   b Buds stalked *Acer* 154
   c Buds pointed; sh winged or
     ribbed *Lagerstroemia* 181

5 Sh squarish, green for 1st winter
   Euonymus 152

6 a Terminal bud lacking   7
   b Terminal bud present   8

7 a Sh slender; buds 3–6 mm,
     crimson-brown *Cercidiphyllum*
     115, see also *Acer* (p160, 161)
   b Sh stouter, over 5 mm; buds small,
     less than 2 mm *Paulownia* 186 or
     Catalpa 187

8 Buds naked *Euodia* 152

9 a Buds have 4–8 pubescent scales
     Fraxinus 182
   b Buds have 8+ scales   10

10 a Sh stout, buds large *Aesculus* 166
   b Sh less stout, buds under 8 mm,
     not resinous *Acer* 154

11 a Shs have spines   12
   b Shs do not have spines   13

12 a Spines brown, curved, paired
     either side of bud *Robinia* 146
   b Spines stout, 3-pronged, often on
     bole *Gleditsia* 146
   c Spines single with buds set at bases
     Crataegus 122, *Mespilus* 123,
     Malus 130, *Pyrus* 133, *Prunus*
     134 (rarely in most except *Crataegus*)

13 a ♂ catkins exposed over winter at
     twig end   14
   b Not as above   16

14 Buds stalked; fr a woody, cone-like
   catkin, persistent *Alnus* 90

15 **a** Sh has bristly hrs; fr a nut *Corylus* 92
   b Sh has no bristly hrs; fr a catkin
   Betula 87

16 **a** Buds naked   17
   b Buds have scales   20

17 **a** Pith chambered *Pterocarya* 85
   b Pith solid   18

18 **a** Sh ribbed, brown *Robinia* 146
   b Sh round   19

19 **a** Sh green *Gleditsia* 146
   b Sh brown or brownish *Rhus* 150

20 **a** Buds have single outer scale   21
   b Buds with 2+ scales   24

21 **a** Lf scar around bud   22
   b Lf scar only below bud   23

22 **a** Bud conic, single *Platanus* 153
   b Buds adpressed, usually 2+
   together *Styrax* 180
   c Bud spine-shaped,
   1–1.5 cm, *Tetracentron* 106

23 **a** Terminal bud large, pinched at
   base *Magnolia* 116
   b Terminal lacking, other buds conic,
   adpressed *Salix* 79

24 Winter buds clustered at sh end; elsewhere spaced, fewer, smaller *Quercus* 98

25 **a** Bud single, central on short sh   26
   b Buds multiple *or* shs not short   27

26 **a** Sh ribbed; fr a persistent cone
   Larix 52
   b Sh round; fr a drupe *Gingko* 21

27 Bud spindle-shaped, pointed, 2 cm
   Fagus 94

28 Fr 4-winged *Halesia* 181

29 Pith chambered *Juglans* 84

30 Bud acute, adpressed *Carpinus* 93
   or *Nothofagus* 96

31 Bud resinous *Populus* 73, *Sorbus* 124

32 **a** Bud stalked   33
   b Bud sessile   34

33 **a** Bark flakes to pink or yellow-green
   below *Parrotia* 120
   b Bark tight, regularly ridged
   Liriodendron 119

The conifers

The Gymnospermae, known colloquially as the conifers, belong to three different botanical groups or orders: the Gingko group, the Yew group and the true conifers. Britain has only three native conifers, the Scots pine, the Yew and the Juniper, many other species which are now familiar having been introduced from Europe, Asia and America. The simple upright habit, making good timber, and the fact that they can grow fast on poor soils and in harsh climates have made conifers ideal for widespread forestry cultivation.

The fundamental botanical difference between conifers and all others plants is that their ovules, which develop into seeds, are carried naked. This gives the group their scientific name, the Gymnospermae, and distinguishes them from the Angiospermae or "enclosed ovule" trees, known as broadleaf trees. The ovules are borne on the scales of the female flower, an immature cone, which closes its scales after fertilization.

This is of little help with identification, however, and it is far better to examine other characteristics of growth, habit and fruit. Conifers in general have a strongly monopodal growth habit, with a single stem and much lighter, smaller side branches. Some do not maintain this character into old age and particularly in European larch and the silver firs one or two very heavy horizontal side branches may turn up at the ends and form competing leaders. Some of the yews also have a tendency to heavier branching; forking often occurs and one of the stems outpaces and suppresses the other.

The illustrations above show some points to look for when examining the superficially similar needles of most conifers. The spruce needle a has a pointed apex, is squarish in section, and is usually similar in appearance above and below. The Silver fir needle b and c is notched at the apex, much flatter, and has white bands on the underside which are in fact the stomata, pores which open and close as the light intensity and humidity vary. Conifer leaves are generally arranged helically along the shoot, although this is sometimes disguised when the leaves are twisted at the base and appear to be arranged pectinately, spreading either side of the shoot. In some species the leaves may be arranged on short shoots, most notably amongst the cedars, larches and gingko. Although still in a helix the leaves are compressed and appear to be a whorl with a central bud.

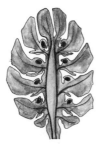

The seeds are ripe in the autumn six or eighteen months after fertilization, and the cone scales usually open, in dry weather, to release them on the wind. The seeds are tucked between the fertile and bract scales (left).

They are usually winged to assist in their distribution. The number of seeds per scale can vary from one to as many as twenty. On some conifers the seeds remain attached to the scales, which themselves separate from the cone and fall.

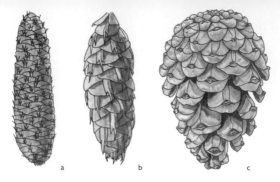

a   b   c

The colloquial name of the conifers derives from the cones, the hard woody fruits with overlapping scales which bear their seeds. They vary enormously from one genus to another, and are perhaps the best means of identification; the illustrations on this page show some points to look for. The Silver fir cone **a** sits erect on the shoot, and is long and cylindrical. It is also distinctive because of the bracts, which are reflexed, and stand out from the body of the cone. This is one of the cones which are rarely found whole on the ground, because their scales are deciduous, falling to the ground and leaving a long bare stalk or rachis on the tree. The Douglas fir cone **b** is equally distinctive in its growth, as it always hangs from the shoot. It is also shorter and more ovoid in shape, and has prominent bracts, which are three-pointed. The pine cone **c**, with its rounded base, pointed tip and triangular scales, is often imagined to be typical of all cones, although it only reaches this form after 18–30 months in *P. pinea,* as illustrated. A feature of these cones is the blunt projection known as an umbo, borne on the outside of each scale. Pine cones are often asymmetrical.

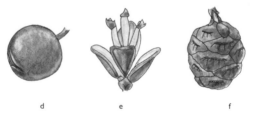

d   e   f

The Juniper fruit **d** is quite unlike that of any other conifer, in that it is not really a cone at all but a soft fleshy berry. As the fruit takes two or three years to ripen, the green immature fruit and the ripe blue ones can usually be found on the same female tree. The female flowers begin life like all other conifers, as open scales, but they mature into hard round berries, recognizable by the scars and blunt points left from what were their scales. The Western red cedar cone **e** is unusual in not having overlapping scales, but ones which separate from the base. The centre of the cone is leathery and ovoid, visible behind the few spreading scales. The cone of the Coast redwood **f** is much smaller and very knobbly, with the scales presenting a diamond-shaped surface. These scales, peltate with a central stalk, each have a central hollow, and as they ripen from green to brown they shrink and separate. The seeds, which can easily be obtained by shaking a newly ripened cone, vary considerably in size and appearance.

Gingko family *Gingkoaceae*
Gingko

Gingko biloba

30m. Crown columnar, broadening with age. **Branches** short, numerous, dipping when old. **Bark** ridged, fissured

Buds set spirally around shoots

Leaves variable, from 6–12cm, set in whorls of 2–5 on short, slow-growing, older shoots; larger, set singly on new shoots. **Blades** open pale yellow green, golden in autumn

Veins straight, parallel, non-dividing

Leaf ribbed, divided into 2 or more lobes on soft shoots; those on long shoots may be undivided

The Gingko is the only survivor of a group of trees that flourished some 200 million years ago. Its primitive ancestry shows in its regular, dichotomous (forked) venation and the rudimentary method by which its ovule is fertilized. As in the ferns, this is by free-swimming sperm cells and fertilization often occurs *after* its ovoid, yellow fruit, found only on female trees, has fallen. This emits a putrid stench once its fleshy coat begins to rot. The Gingko is only native to a remote part of China where it was adopted as a sacred tree by Buddhist monks who carried it to Japan. From there it was introduced to Europe and America in the eighteenth century. Specimens planted then still survive and an immunity to air pollution and most pests and diseases makes Gingko ideal for towns. Its name, 'Maidenhair tree', is based on the similarity of its leaves to those of Maidenhair fern.

Yew family *Taxaceae*

Yews are usually dioecious; females produce solitary seeds in a fleshy aril. Leaves are set spirally or in pectinate ranks.

Yew

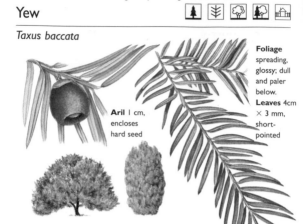

Taxus baccata

Foliage spreading, glossy; dull and paler below.
Leaves 4cm × 3 mm, short-pointed

Aril 1 cm, encloses hard seed

50m. Crown dense, on several stems. **Bark** scaly

Irish yew (*T. baccata* 'Fastigiata'), usually ♀

A widespread species native to chalk upland and shady, broad-leaved woods, the Yew is noted for its longevity – many in churchyards may be 1000 years old – and its scarlet "berries" which ripen in September and are distributed by birds.

California nutmeg

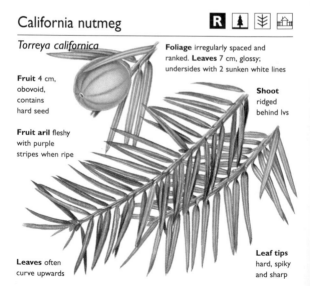

Torreya californica

Foliage irregularly spaced and ranked. **Leaves** 7 cm, glossy; undersides with 2 sunken white lines

Fruit 4 cm, obovoid, contains hard seed

Shoot ridged behind lvs

Fruit aril fleshy with purple stripes when ripe

Leaves often curve upwards

Leaf tips hard, spiky and sharp

An open-crowned tree with spreading branches and stout shoots, this species reaches 15 metres and its fruit has seeds resembling those of the true nutmeg. Japanese nutmeg (*T. nucifera*) has shorter and decurrent needles.

Podocarp family *Podocarpaceae*

These species come mainly from the southern hemisphere and carry cones with fleshy scales and less regular foliage than the yew family. Male and female flowers may appear on the same tree.

Prince Albert yew

R ♠ ⅄ ⌂

Saxegothaea conspicua

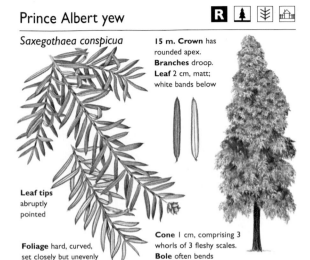

15 m. Crown has rounded apex.
Branches droop.
Leaf 2 cm, matt; white bands below

Leaf tips abruptly pointed

Foliage hard, curved, set closely but unevenly

Cone 1 cm, comprising 3 whorls of 3 fleshy scales.
Bole often bends

A Chilean tree which was named after Queen Victoria's consort, this differs from Yew in its fruit, irregular foliage and leaf undersides while its less dense, pendulous shoots distinguish it from *Prumnopitys andinus*.

Chilean yew

R ♠ ⅄ ⌂

Prumnopitys andinus (syn. *Podocarpus andinus*)

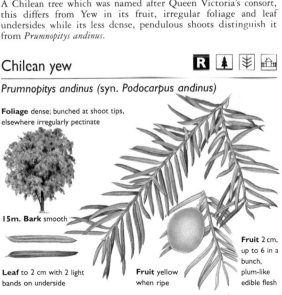

Foliage dense; bunched at shoot tips, elsewhere irregularly pectinate

15m. Bark smooth

Leaf to 2 cm with 2 light bands on underside

Fruit yellow when ripe

Fruit 2 cm, up to 6 in a bunch, plum-like edible flesh

This tree of variable habit is sometimes confused with Prince Albert yew but is closer to Willow podocarp (*Podocarpus salignus*) which has 5–10 cm leaves parted in two ranks and a red-brown shaggy bark. Both these podocarps are native to Chile.

23

Chile pine family *Araucariaceae*

This family comprises three genera and 37 species, all natives of the southern hemisphere. Trees are either male or female, the female ones carrying globose or ovoid cones containing many scales, each with one seed. Leaves are hard with parallel venation and are usually broad and arranged spirally.

Monkey puzzle

Araucaria araucana

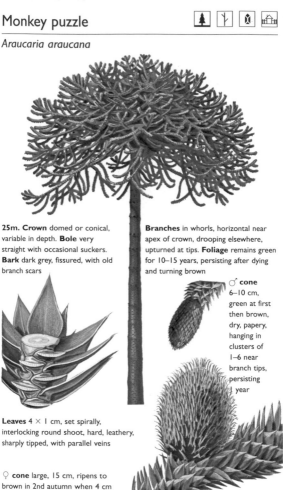

25m. Crown domed or conical, variable in depth. **Bole** very straight with occasional suckers. **Bark** dark grey, fissured, with old branch scars

Branches in whorls, horizontal near apex of crown, drooping elsewhere, upturned at tips. **Foliage** remains green for 10–15 years, persisting after dying and turning brown

♂ **cone** 6–10 cm, green at first then brown, dry, papery, hanging in clusters of 1–6 near branch tips, persisting 1 year

Leaves 4 × 1 cm, set spirally, interlocking round shoot, hard, leathery, sharply tipped, with parallel veins

♀ **cone** large, 15 cm, ripens to brown in 2nd autumn when 4 cm seeds released as it breaks up

Indigenous to Chile where its tasty seeds were once an important food of the Araucano tribe, the Monkey puzzle was first introduced to Europe in 1794 and its common name, alluding to the problems its sharp foliage would give potential climbers, was first used in 1834. The Norfolk Island pine (*A. heterophylla*) has softer, awl-shaped leaves. It can grow in the open in warm areas but is more common as an indoor plant.

Cypress family *Cupressaceae*

Trees in the Cypress family are distinguished from other conifers, except *Metasequoia* (p 38), by their paired or ternate leaves. Those of juvenile plants are always awl-shaped, a condition retained by some species and many cultivars. Adult leaves are mostly small, scale-like and adpressed. Members of Cupressaceae carry male and female flowers on the same or separate trees and three types of cone are produced: those of *Cupressus* (pp 25–7 and 29) and *Chamaecyparis* (pp 28–31) are globose or ellipsoid with peltate scales; those of *Juniperus* (pp 34–5) have unique fleshy scales which are fused together. All other Cypress genera – including *Thuja* (pp 32–3), *Thujopsis* (p 33) and *Calocedrus* (p 34) – have larger cones with woody scales hinged at their bases.

Monterey cypress

Cupressus macrocarpa

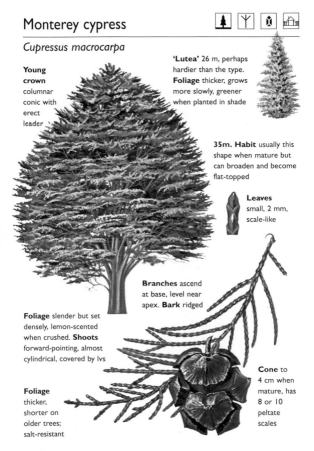

Young crown columnar conic with erect leader

'Lutea' 26 m, perhaps hardier than the type. **Foliage** thicker, grows more slowly, greener when planted in shade

35m. Habit usually this shape when mature but can broaden and become flat-topped

Leaves small, 2 mm, scale-like

Branches ascend at base, level near apex. **Bark** ridged

Foliage slender but set densely, lemon-scented when crushed. **Shoots** forward-pointing, almost cylindrical, covered by lvs

Foliage thicker, shorter on older trees; salt-resistant

Cone to 4 cm when mature, has 8 or 10 peltate scales

This species is found wild on the coast of California and was widely planted as a hedge tree although it has now been largely superseded in that role by the hardier and faster-growing Leyland cypress (p 27). A fungal disease, *Seiridium* (= *Coryneum*) *cardinale*, attacks Monterey cypress as well as Italian cypress (p 26) and can prove fatal.

Italian cypress

Cupressus sempervirens

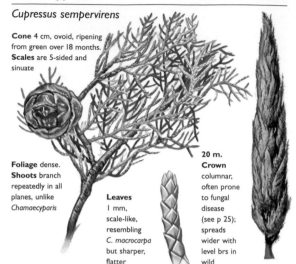

Cone 4 cm, ovoid, ripening from green over 18 months.
Scales are 5-sided and sinuate

Foliage dense.
Shoots branch repeatedly in all planes, unlike *Chamaecyparis*

Leaves
1 mm, scale-like, resembling *C. macrocarpa* but sharper, flatter

**20 m.
Crown** columnar, often prone to fungal disease (see p 25); spreads wider with level brs in wild

This classic cypress, native from Greece and the Balkans to Iran, is now widely distributed throughout Mediterranean countries. Cedar of Goa (*C. lusitanica*), from Mexico, has a broader crown, smaller, glaucous cones and spreading, pointed leaves.

Smooth cypress

Cupressus glabra

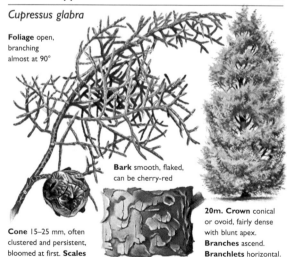

Foliage open, branching almost at 90°

Bark smooth, flaked, can be cherry-red

Cone 15–25 mm, often clustered and persistent, bloomed at first. **Scales** have low, curved spikes

20m. Crown conical or ovoid, fairly dense with blunt apex.
Branches ascend.
Branchlets horizontal.
Bole short

Distinguished by its bark, this tree is being increasingly planted as an ornamental. It was once classified as a cultivar of Arizona cypress (*C. arizonica*) whose bark is much rougher.

Leyland cypress

Cupressus x leylandii (syn. *Cupressocyparis leylandii*)

Cone
(when present)
3 cm, globular,
brown

Foliage dark green or grey, in irregular flattish planes which is often nodding to one side, less dense near leader. **Shoots** branch repeatedly. **Leaves** slightly incurved with ridged glands. **Growth** fast, can exceed 1 m a year

40m. Crown dense, columnar with conic or rounded conic apex. **Branches** ascend steeply. **Leader** leans slightly, not drooping as in Lawson cypress (pp 30–31). **Bark** initially smooth, then ridged becoming stringy

'Castlewellan' is extremely vigorous and its foliage, arranged in plumes, turns bronze-green in winter

Leyland cypress is a hybrid of Monterey cypress (p 25) and Nootka cypress (p 29) and the qualities inherited from its parents – the vigorous growth rate of the first and the adaptable durability of the second – have made this tree unbeatable as a hedge conifer. Several clones are now marketed. The most popular, 'Haggerston Grey', was first raised in 1888 but two recently introduced golden forms, 'Castlewellan' and 'Robinson's Gold' are becoming increasingly acceptable. Leyland does not set viable seed but plants are easily raised from cuttings.

Hinoki cypress

Chamaecyparis obtusa

Foliage in very flat sprays

Foliage in fan-like, feathery sprays. **Leaves** small, 2 mm, in blunt pairs, with white scale joints on undersides

25m. Crown columnar, conic. **Branches** level then ascending. **Bole** straight. **Bark** fissured

Cone 1 cm

This native of Japan can be distinguished from other "false" cypresses by its blunt, incurved leaves and larger, round cones. 'Crippsii', a popular cultivar, has bright, golden-yellow foliage which darkens to green inside the crown.

Sawara cypress

Chamaecyparis pisifera

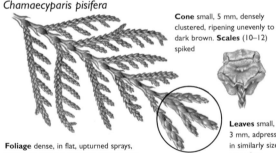

Cone small, 5 mm, densely clustered, ripening unevenly to dark brown. **Scales** (10–12) spiked

Leaves small, 3 mm, adpressed, in similarly sized pairs, fine-pointed, incurved

Foliage dense, in flat, upturned sprays, darkening with age and with bright white leaf bases below

Leaves of many Sawara cultivars are always awl-shaped and set in pairs. Those of **'Squarrosa'** (right) 6 mm long while leaves of **'Plumosa'** are half this size

Native to Japan, this tree has distinctively small cones and the type is far less common than its numerous cultivars. These can be divided into those with pendulous foliage such as 'Filifera' and those whose awl-shaped leaves are set at about 45° like 'Plumosa' or approximately at right angles as on 'Squarrosa'.

Nootka cypress

Cupressus nootkatensis (syn. *Chamaecyparis nootkatensis*)

Leading shoot leans

Crown is extremely regular

Cone 1 cm, globular, with large scale spikes, green with blue bloom, ripens brown over 2 years

Foliage very pendulous, in thick, flat, alternate sprays. **Leaves** 2–3 mm, hard, in equal-sized pairs

30 cm. Bark stringy, peels

Sometimes classified as a *Chamaecyparis*. It is a parent of Leyland cypress (p 27) and is easily recognized by its hanging branchlets and the hooked spines of its cones. 'Pendula' has very pendulous foliage with shorter, upturned branches and 2 cm cones.

White cypress

Chamaecyparis thyoides

Foliage very slender, 1 mm, short, fern-like, angular green or bluish-grey sprays. **Cones** set on small branchlets

15m. Crown columnar or broad conic. **Branches** short. **Bark** stringy. **Cone** 6 mm, glaucous blue-purple ripening brown

Leaves often have central resin glands and carry prominent white marks near bases, particularly on undersides

Leaves very small, down to 1 mm, acutely pointed, incurved and close-pressed but freer on vigorous growth. **Shoot** becomes brown in 2nd year

The slow-growing White cypress is native to swamps along the eastern American seaboard. Its wood is so durable trees buried for decades have proved sufficiently strong to use for making roof shingles. Its botanical name comes from a resemblance to *Thuja* (pp 32–3) and its common name from the paleness of its foliage.

Lawson cypress

Chamaecyparis lawsoniana

20–35 m, to 50m in wild. **Crown** regular in young trees, less so in mature ones. **Stem** often forked. **Foliage** dense, pendulous, becoming spaced in old trees. **Leader** and new shoots always droop. **Terminals** wispy, unbranched near tips

Cones 8 mm, globose, ripening from green or blue-green to dark brown. **Scales** (8) have short central spikes

Bark smooth, ridged then scaly, dark red-brown, purplish on older trees

♂ **flowers** terminate weakest branchlets

Foliage flat, fern-like. **Leaves** grouped in pairs: lateral ones keel-shaped, facing pairs smaller, adpressed. Each leaf has central translucent gland. Between leaf scales, stomata form thin, white lines. Especially clear on foliage underside, giving best identification features

The Lawson cypress is native to a small area on the Oregon–California border and as a forest species is characterized by a uniform crown of dense, pendent foliage. An expedition sponsored by the Scottish nurseryman Peter Lawson, discovered it there in 1854 and the vast array of hardy and easily propagated cultivars raised since then – some 250 – have made this "false" cypress the most common ornamental conifer now grown. Its varieties can be divided into a group with vivid foliage, one with distinctly shaped habits and a third whose long, awl-like leaves resemble the juvenile leaves of the seedling.

Some cultivars of Lawson cypress

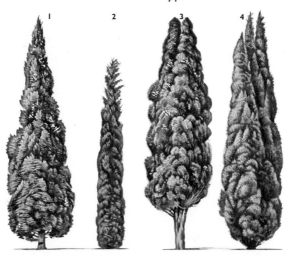

1 **'Allumii'**: 20m; compact habit, soft foliage. 2 **'Columnaris'**: 10m; dense, consistently narrow crown. 3 **'Erecta'**: 25m; first Lawson cypress cultivar, raised in 1855 from seeds of a Californian type; much-forked crown. 4 **'Fletcherii'**: 16m; juvenile foliage, often on several stems; multiple leaders.

5 **'Intertexta'**: 25m; foliage sparse, dark and bloomed, sprays pendent. 6 **'Lutea'**: 16m; short, pendulous branchlets; older interior foliage darker. 7 **'Stewartii'** : 16m; ascending branches with sprays decurved below shoot. 8 **'Wissellii'**: 25m; spaced foliage arranged in dense, radiating "spires".

Western red cedar

Thuja plicata

40m. Crown conic, broadening with age. **Tip** erect

Cone 1cm, with 10–12 scales, has hooked tip, flask-shaped when closed

Seed 5mm, winged, notched

Branches light, even, upswept at ends, can layer in old trees

Foliage aromatic

Bole fluted

Bark dull, stringy

Foliage flattened, overlapping. **Leaves** incurved, glossy, paler below with whitish streaks

From the Pacific coast of North America, this majestic tree has a light but very even crown and is planted for its light and durable timber, often used for roofing shingles. Japanese thuja (*T. standishii*) has lighter, blunt, glanded leaves which smell of lemons.

Chinese thuja

Platycodus orientalis (syn. *Thuja orientalis*)

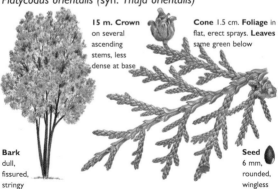

15 m. Crown on several ascending stems, less dense at base

Cone 1.5 cm. **Foliage** in flat, erect sprays. **Leaves** same green below

Bark dull, fissured, stringy

Seed 6 mm, rounded, wingless

This species is often included in the *Thuja* genus and although its foliage bears some resemblance to that of the true thujas, it differs from them in its broader, glaucous cones which have fewer, strongly hooked scales and large, round, wingless seeds.

32

White cedar

Thuja occidentalis

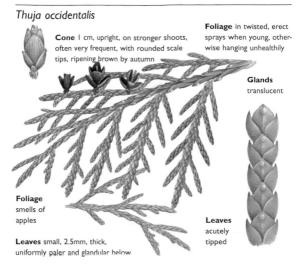

Cone 1 cm, upright, on stronger shoots, often very frequent, with rounded scale tips, ripening brown by autumn

Foliage in twisted, erect sprays when young, otherwise hanging unhealthily

Glands translucent

Foliage smells of apples

Leaves acutely tipped

Leaves small, 2.5mm, thick, uniformly paler and glandular below

Small and slow-growing, this species was introduced to Europe from eastern North America, perhaps as early as 1536. Its smooth cones and foliage underside are distinctive. 'Lutea' has a denser crown and stronger branches whose tips bear golden leaves.

Hiba

R

Thujopsis dolabrata

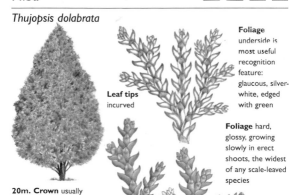

Foliage underside is most useful recognition feature: glaucous, silver-white, edged with green

Leaf tips incurved

Foliage hard, glossy, growing slowly in erect shoots, the widest of any scale-leaved species

20m. Crown usually conic on several stems. **Bark** finely shredded

Leaves large, broad, to 7 × 4mm

'Variegata' has some cream-green shoots

This Japanese tree rarely grows on a single stem and carries rounded, blue-grey cones. The leaf undersides of Korean thuja (*Thuja koraiensis*) are also – sometimes completely – silvery glaucous but its foliage is softer and has typical *Thuja* cones.

Incense cedar

Calocedrus decurrens

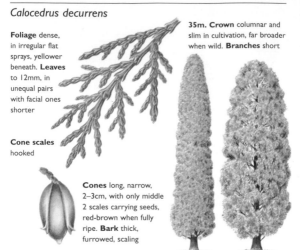

Foliage dense, in irregular flat sprays, yellower beneath. **Leaves** to 12mm, in unequal pairs with facial ones shorter

Cone scales hooked

Cones long, narrow, 2–3cm, with only middle 2 scales carrying seeds, red-brown when fully ripe. **Bark** thick, furrowed, scaling

35m. Crown columnar and slim in cultivation, far broader when wild. **Branches** short

A native of Oregon and California, Incense cedar can be confused with the much more common 'Erecta' cultivar of Lawson cypress (p 31) but is distinguished by its irregular foliage, short, upswept branches with unequal pairs of leaves which are yellow beneath. Its fragrant timber gives the tree its name.

Juniper

Juniperus communis

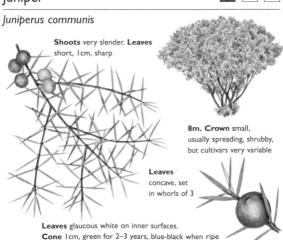

Shoots very slender. **Leaves** short, 1cm, sharp

8m. Crown small, usually spreading, shrubby, but cultivars very variable

Leaves concave, set in whorls of 3

Leaves glaucous white on inner surfaces.
Cone 1cm, green for 2–3 years, blue-black when ripe

Juniper will grow on both acid and alkaline sites and has a very wide distribution throughout the northern hemisphere. The bright green leaves of Temple juniper (*J. rigida*) are softer and longer while Alerce (*Fitzroya cuppressoides*) has spreading blue-green leaves with two silver bands on each side.

Pencil cedar

Juniperus virginiana

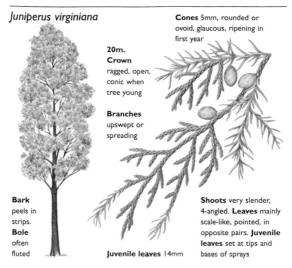

Cones 5mm, rounded or ovoid, glaucous, ripening in first year

**20m.
Crown** ragged, open, conic when tree young

Branches upswept or spreading

Bark peels in strips.
Bole often fluted

Juvenile leaves 14mm

Shoots very slender, 4-angled. **Leaves** mainly scale-like, pointed, in opposite pairs. **Juvenile leaves** set at tips and bases of sprays

Pencil juniper, the tallest of the junipers, is indigenous to eastern North America and provides useful timber, especially for pencils. While not dissimilar to Chinese juniper, its finer foliage, *paired* juvenile leaves, *pointed* scale leaves and much smaller cones clearly distinguish it.

Chinese juniper

Juniperus chinensis

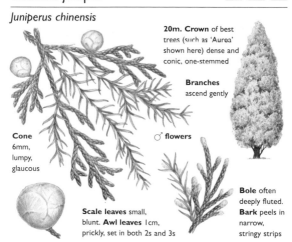

20m. Crown of best trees (such as 'Aurea' shown here) dense and conic, one-stemmed

Branches ascend gently

♂ **flowers**

Cone 6mm, lumpy, glaucous

Scale leaves small, blunt. **Awl leaves** 1cm, prickly, set in both 2s and 3s

Bole often deeply fluted. **Bark** peels in narrow, stringy strips

Chinese juniper is the most common juniper growing as a tree and of its several cultivars, 'Aurea' is the most popular and produces masses of male flowers. Drooping juniper (*J. recurva*) has dry, pendent foliage which rustles when shaken; its softer, green, adpressed awl leaves are set in threes.

35

Redwood family *Taxodiaceae*

This ancient group of large, beautiful trees comprises 10 genera from North America, eastern Asia and Tasmania. Its members usually have evergreen leaves, which are flat, linear or awl-shaped and set helically along the shoot, and globular woody cones, whose peltate scales are also arranged helically. All redwoods are monoecious. They have thick barks that are red-brown and fibrous. Three genera are deciduous.

Wellingtonia

Sequoiadendron giganteum

Leaves small, to 7 mm, awl-shaped, hard, dotted with white stomata

Foliage blue-grey when young then shiny, dark green on older shoots

Shoot stout, initially covered by leaves, later developing grey-brown fissures

Cone large, 4–6 cm, 35–40 scales, green for 2 years, then brown

Branches have tips upswept

50 m. Crown often has rounded apex. **Bole** tapers, fluted. **Bark** often dimpled by Treecreepers using it for winter roosting

Bark very thick, to 30 cm, soft and resilient, can withstand punching

Wellingtonia is the world's largest (though not the tallest) living phenomenon and is native to 72 groves on the high, western slopes of the Californian Sierra Nevadas where it was first discovered in 1841. The largest individual there, named "General Sherman", is 83 m tall, has a trunk diameter of 10 m and weighs 1,000 tonnes, yet must have developed over the centuries from a seed weighing a mere 5 milligrammes. Such specimens may live for 4,000 years although the average age of native species is only a quarter of this. In Europe, growth rates have exceeded 50 m in a century. Wellingtonias have deep roots to withstand long, dry summers and their thick bark gives protection against forest fires.

(California) Redwood

Sequoia sempervirens

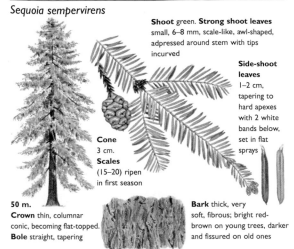

Shoot green. **Strong shoot leaves** small, 6–8 mm, scale-like, awl-shaped, adpressed around stem with tips incurved

Side-shoot leaves 1–2 cm, tapering to hard apexes with 2 white bands below, set in flat sprays

Cone 3 cm. **Scales** (15–20) ripen in first season

50 m. **Crown** thin, columnar conic, becoming flat-topped. **Bole** straight, tapering

Bark thick, very soft, fibrous; bright red-brown on young trees, darker and fissured on old ones

This redwood is the tallest tree in the world, reaching 112 m (the height of St Paul's Cathedral, London) in its native California where it thrives in the damp atmosphere of the narrow, coastal "fogbelt". Chinese fir (*Cunninghamia lanceolata*) has a similar bark but much longer, more broadly based, sharp pointed leaves.

Swamp cypress

Taxodium distichum

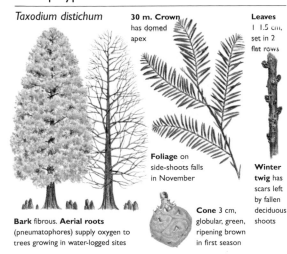

30 m. Crown has domed apex

Leaves 1–1.5 cm, set in 2 flat rows

Foliage on side-shoots falls in November

Winter twig has scars left by fallen deciduous shoots

Bark fibrous. **Aerial roots** (pneumatophores) supply oxygen to trees growing in water-logged sites

Cone 3 cm, globular, green, ripening brown in first season

Sometimes confused with *Metasequoia* (p 38) from which it can be distinguished by its alternate foliage, this tree from the southern USA prefers waterside sites but grows well on any fairly moist soil. The closely related Pond cypress (*T. ascendens*) has erect, spiky shoots of shorter, radially arranged leaves.

Dawn redwood

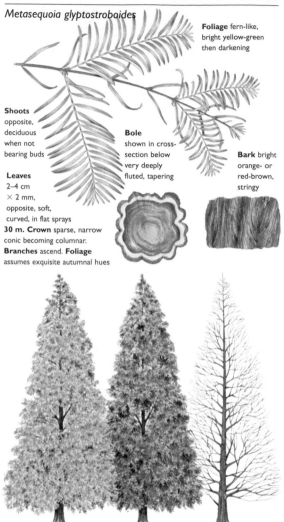

Metasequoia glyptostroboides

Foliage fern-like, bright yellow-green then darkening

Shoots opposite, deciduous when not bearing buds

Bole shown in cross-section below very deeply fluted, tapering

Bark bright orange- or red-brown, stringy

Leaves 2–4 cm × 2 mm, opposite, soft, curved, in flat sprays
30 m. Crown sparse, narrow conic becoming columnar.
Branches ascend. **Foliage** assumes exquisite autumnal hues

Long thought to be extinct, this fine tree was located in southeastern China as recently as 1941, since when its hardiness, the ease with which it propagates and a growth rate which can average a metre per annum have made it a popular ornamental. Its botanical name indicates affinities with *Sequoia* (p 37) and the rare, deciduous Chinese swamp cypress (*Glyptostrobus pensilis*) but it is more easily confused with Swamp cypress (p 37), whose similar foliage is also deciduous. The leaves and lateral shoots of Dawn redwood, however, are longer and *opposite*. It is unique in carrying its side-buds *below* its shoots and not in their axils.

Japanese cedar

Cryptomeria japonica

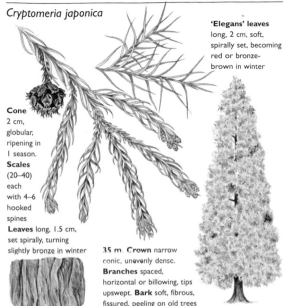

'Elegans' leaves long, 2 cm, soft, spirally set, becoming red or bronze-brown in winter

Cone 2 cm, globular, ripening in 1 season. **Scales** (20–40) each with 4–6 hooked spines

Leaves long, 1.5 cm, set spirally, turning slightly bronze in winter

35 m. Crown narrow conic, unevenly dense. **Branches** spaced, horizontal or billowing, tips upswept. **Bark** soft, fibrous, fissured, peeling on old trees

As an introduced ornamental, this tree never reaches the heights it attains in its native China and Japan. The Tasmanian *Athrotaxis* species have similar cones but shorter leaves: King William pine (*A. selaginoides*) has hard, shiny leaves of 1 cm, Summit cedar (*A. laxifolia*) awl-like ones with free tips to 2 mm and Tasmanian cedar (*A. cupressoides*) adpressed scale leaves.

Japanese umbrella pine

Sciadopitys verticillata

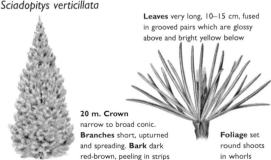

Leaves very long, 10–15 cm, fused in grooved pairs which are glossy above and bright yellow below

20 m. Crown narrow to broad conic. **Branches** short, upturned and spreading. **Bark** dark red-brown, peeling in strips

Foliage set round shoots in whorls

Native to the mountains of Japan, where it is an important timber tree, this species grows very slowly in European parks and large gardens. Its distinctive foliage of long and whorled, glossy "double" leaves distinguishes it. Now often placed in its own family, the Sciadopitaceae.

Pine family *Pinaceae*

The Pine family is the most varied of all those groups of trees which bear cones. Besides the genus *Pinus* itself, the family also contains those of *Abies*, *Picea*, *Tsuga*, *Hesperoperce*, *Pseudotsuga* and *Larix* as well as *Pseudolarix*, *Cathaya*, *Nothotsuga* and *Keteleeria* (these latter four are fairly obscure Chinese genera and, because they are so seldom found elsewhere, not included in this book).

Together, all the Pinaceae comprise well over 250 species, all of which are native to the northern hemisphere. They all have woody cones with spirally arranged scales and linear flat leaves (usually called needles) which are attached to the shoot in a variety of different ways.

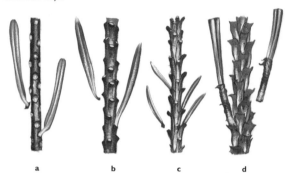

a   b   c   d

The illustrations above demonstrate these differences. The leaves of Silver fir (*Abies*) leave a depressed or concave scar (**a**) while a slightly raised scar, together with a minutely stalked leaf (**b**) shows the tree is almost certainly a Douglas fir (*Pseudotsuga*). Spruces (*Picea*) are immediately notable for the prominent woody peg (*pulvinus*) that is left where the leaf (**c**) falls from it naturally. The leaves of pines (*Pinus*) are set in fascicles of two, three or five and bound by a basal sheath (**d**). These fascicles are extensions of short or spur shoots and – despite the number of their leaves – can always be brought together to make up a simple, but divided cylinder. This adaptation probably allows the leaves to maximize their surface for photosynthesis while controlling transpiration.

The length of the shoot can also be a guide to genus; while all the family produce long shoots, some genera, namely the pines, larches (*Larix*) and cedars (*Cedrus*) also produce much shorter shoots. These grow from a bud in the axil of a needle on a long shoot, and eventually a new whorl of needles is formed. The bud in the centre of this new whorl may either be the starting point for subsequent growth or may remain dormant for years. The shorter shoots of the larches grow for several years and have many deciduous needles, a feature shared with *Pseudolarix*.

The majority of trees in Pinaceae grow pendent cones but *Abies*, *Cedrus* and *Larix* have cones which remain erect after the female flowers have been fertilized. Silver fir and Cedar cones break apart to release their seeds, leaving the central core of these cones, a long spike or "candle", left standing on the shoot while Larches have persistent woody cones.

All other genera have pendent cones whose scales remain attached to their central axis and eventually fall to the ground intact.

Silver firs *Abies*

So-called because of the undersides of their foliage, most Silver firs have short leaves set in flat ranks which become more assurgent in the upper crown. Their deciduous cones develop at the top of the tree. About 40 species may be encountered.

Silver fir

Abies alba

Cone 10–15 cm, green ripening brown. **Bracts** pointed, reflexed. **Leaves** 2.5 cm, with white stomata below

Foliage well parted. **Shoot** with dark or blackish pubescence

50 m. Crown slender and open. **Branches** spreading, whorled. **Bole** long

Silver fir is an important forest tree and common in the mountains of central Europe. It has thick leaves with notched tips, and non-resinous buds. King Boris fir (*A. borisii-regis*) has denser foliage, narrower leaves to 3 cm and pale-haired twigs.

Caucasian fir

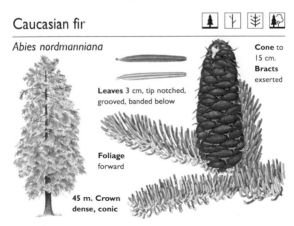

Abies nordmanniana

Cone to 15 cm. **Bracts** exserted

Leaves 3 cm, tip notched, grooved, banded below

Foliage forward

45 m. Crown dense, conic

This fir has a more luxuriant crown than *A. alba* and its forward-pointing foliage persists for about 6–8 years. Bornmüller fir (*A. bornmülleriana*) has longer leaves with spots of stomata by the upperside tips, shiny red-brown shoots and sticky buds.

41

Spanish fir

Abies pinsapo

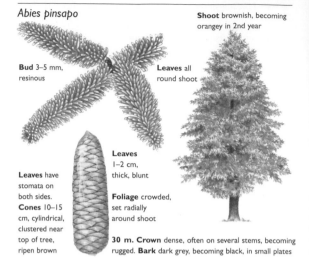

Shoot brownish, becoming orangey in 2nd year

Bud 3–5 mm, resinous

Leaves all round shoot

Leaves have stomata on both sides. **Cones** 10–15 cm, cylindrical, clustered near top of tree, ripen brown

Leaves 1–2 cm, thick, blunt

Foliage crowded, set radially around shoot

30 m. Crown dense, often on several stems, becoming rugged. **Bark** dark grey, becoming black, in small plates

Spanish fir only occurs wild in southern Spain but is fairly widely planted in Europe. It is also called Hedgehog fir because of its stiff foliage; that of Algerian fir (*A. numidica*) is similar but is parted below and has a prominent band of stomata at its leaf tips.

Greek fir

Abies cephalonica

Cone to 15 cm. **Bracts** exserted, reflexed

Cones numerous on upper branches

Buds resinous

40 m. Crown conic. **Bark** fissured

Tips spiny

Leaves to 3 cm

Foliage glossy above, silvery-white below, set radially, less dense below

With a massive bole and heavy branches which sometimes rise as secondary leaders, Greek fir is often the bulkiest of the silver firs. *A. cephalonica* var. *apollonis* has denser, blunter, forward-pointing leaves, mostly arranged above the shoot.

Abies concolor • A. concolor var. lowiana

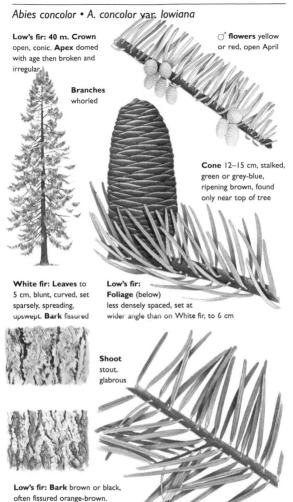

Low's fir: 40 m. Crown open, conic. **Apex** domed with age then broken and irregular

♂ **flowers** yellow or red, open April

Branches whorled

Cone 12–15 cm, stalked, green or grey-blue, ripening brown, found only near top of tree

White fir: Leaves to 5 cm, blunt, curved, set sparsely, spreading, upswept. **Bark** fissured

Low's fir: Foliage (below) less densely spaced, set at wider angle than on White fir, to 6 cm

Shoot stout, glabrous

Low's fir: Bark brown or black, often fissured orange-brown. **Shoot** pale brown or bright green, turning copper-brown or orange-brown in 2nd year

White fir grows wild in the western USA and parts of Mexico, and is recognizable by its long, assurgent, bluish leaves which smell of lemons when crushed. Low's fir, from Oregon and California, has longer leaves which either spread flat or rise on both sides to form a wide U-shaped "groove", thus combining several features of White fir, which grows to the south of its range, with several of Grand fir, which is native further north. Low's fir is ultimately distinguishable from other silver firs by the combination of lax, bluish leaves with a fissured bark usually resembling that of Douglas fir (p 49).

43

Grand fir

Abies grandis

Foliage flat on shoots.
Leaves 5 cm.
Buds 2 mm, conic, grey-white, and resinous

60 m.
Crown conic

Bracts included, later cracked

Cone 9 cm, tapering resinous, ripening brown
Bracts included

Branches whorled, usually level.
Bark smooth, shiny when young with resin blister, later cracked

A very fast-growing species, Grand fir is an important forest tree from western North America, identified by its flat foliage which becomes more assurgent in the upper crown. West Himalayan fir (*A. pindrow*) has large globular buds and longer leaves to 9 cm, spreading down at the sides of its glabrous, ash-grey shoots.

Pacific fir

Abies amabilis

Leaves 3 cm, glossy, curved, grooved, forward-pointing

Cone 15 × 15 cm, smooth.
Bracts included

Leaves silver-banded below

Foliage spreading below

The shapely crown and rich foliage of this fir justify its specific name which may be translated as "lovely". It is native from British Columbia to California. Maries fir (*A. mariesii*) is its closest relative and its 2 cm leaves are glossier. Its shoot has dense orange-red, not light brown, pubescence.

Noble fir

Abies procera (syn. A. nobilis)

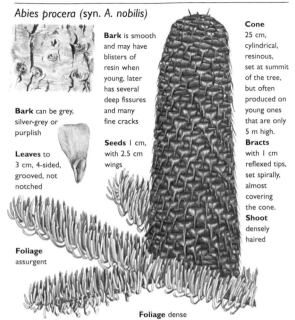

Bark is smooth and may have blisters of resin when young, later has several deep fissures and many fine cracks

Bark can be grey, silver-grey or purplish

Leaves to 3 cm, 4-sided, grooved, not notched

Seeds 1 cm, with 2.5 cm wings

Foliage assurgent

Foliage dense

Cone 25 cm, cylindrical, resinous, set at summit of the tree, but often produced on young ones that are only 5 m high.

Bracts with 1 cm reflexed tips, set spirally, almost covering the cone.

Shoot densely haired

Noble fir is remarkable for the size of its cones, which may contain up to 1,000 seeds and for its silvery fissured mature bark. Its lower branches carry many crimson male flowers in spring.

Red fir

Abies magnifica

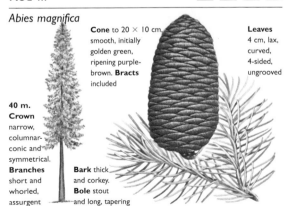

Cone to 20 × 10 cm, smooth, initially golden green, ripening purple-brown. **Bracts** included

Leaves 4 cm, lax, curved, 4-sided, ungrooved

40 m. Crown narrow, columnar-conic and symmetrical.
Branches short and whorled, assurgent

Bark thick and corky.
Bole stout and long, tapering

This fir is native to Oregon and California and while closely related to Noble fir, has ungrooved, longer and less densely set foliage. Its name comes from the red bark of mature trees. The cones of Shasta fir (*A. magnifica* var. *shastensis*) have exserted bracts.

Veitch fir

Abies veitchii

Cone 8 cm, cylindrical, flat-topped, purple-blue initially, ripens brown, smoothly wrinkled

Foliage all pointing forwards, spreading below, rising at 45° to shoot above

Bud 3 mm, shiny, red-purple

Bark dark grey-green, with white patches on old trees

Leaves 3 cm, grey-green above, silver-white below, square-tipped

Bracts slightly exserted

Shoot slightly ribbed, has brown hairs when young. **Foliage** set densely

Veitch fir forms trees to 20 m with tapered, flat-topped crowns. On trees whose crowns reach the ground the lowest branches are very upswept revealing the silver underside of their foliage. It is a native of Japan, as is Sakhalin fir (*A. sachalinensis*), with longer, narrower, bright green leaves to 3.5 cm.

Korean fir

Abies koreana

15 m. Crown conic with slightly ascending branches. **Leaves** spreading below shoot, curving upwards above

Leaves 1–1.5 cm, glossy green or yellow-green above, tips often white

Bark shiny, dark brown to black, smooth, spotted conspicuously with lenticels. **Leaves** vividly white underneath, rather radial and spaced along the fawn shoot

Buds small, globular, initially pale brown but soon covered with white resin. Male cones yellow, 1–1.5 cm

Cone 7 cm, pointed, purple, ripening brown. **Bracts** reflexed, clearly exserted

This silver fir, first discovered in 1907 on Chejv island off Korea, usually only manages to grow to 10 m in 40 years. It is very free in producing its small violet cones, often as a young tree less than 1 m tall. The strongly exserted and reflexed bracts show how cone scales in the Pine family are helically and radially arranged.

Abies forrestii var. forrestii • A. forrestii var. smithii

Forrest fir cone (right) is 7–12 cm long, cylindrical or barrel-shaped, top dimpled, violet, ripening brown over winter. **Bracts** exserted, often reflexed with very prominent awl-like cusps to 5 mm

Smith fir cone (right) often larger, occasionally to 15 cm, **Bracts** exserted, with cusps up to 1 cm, pointing upright except near base of cone. **Bract edges** well exposed, bright blue-purple with light brown edges

Forrest fir shoot (below) stout, red-brown, usually glabrous and finely roughened; in second year deeper colour with pale fissures. **Foliage** may be radial

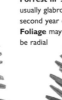

Smith fir shoot (above) brownish orange, with a dense, short pubescence of the same colour. **Leaves** close more over top of shoot. **Foliage** short, perpendicular

Forrest foliage (left) to 4 cm, spreading around shoot, often lax below, dense and may be parted. **Leaf** green above, white below

Smith fir leaves (left) shorter, to 2.5 cm, off-white below, grey bloomed above

This fir was discovered in China and introduced into Britain by George Forrest, after whom it is named. Smith fir is chiefly distinguished by its densely pubescent shoots and longer cusps, and although both trees grow to 25 m, Smith fir has a more columnar and denser crown than Forrest fir. Related species from the Himalayas and west China include Himalayan fir (*A. spectabilis*), which has ash-grey or light brown shoots pubescent in deep grooves and Delavay fir (*A. delavayi*) which has bright violet narrow cones, maroon shoots, orange buds, and inrolled leaf margins which make the leaves narrow and square-tipped. Farges fir (*A. fargesii*) has stout 2.5 cm needles on glossy, purple shoots and conic, purple buds.

Nikko fir

Abies homolepis

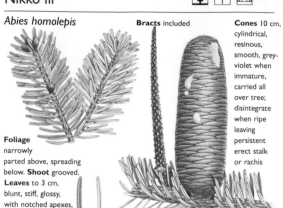

Bracts included

Cones 10 cm, cylindrical, resinous, smooth, grey-violet when immature, carried all over tree; disintegrate when ripe leaving persistent erect stalk or rachis

Foliage narrowly parted above, spreading below. **Shoot** grooved.
Leaves to 3 cm, blunt, stiff, glossy, with notched apexes, grooved, with 2 silvery bands below

Nikko fir, tolerant of urban pollution, has strongly ridged and grooved glabrous shoots. Min fir (*A. recurvata*) has smooth shoots, more ovoid, 8 cm cones, and bluntly pointed needles, green on both surfaces, that may point backwards.

Santa Lucia fir

Abies bracteata

Foliage parted, forward-pointing, widely spaced.
Shoot stout, glabrous, almost shiny, green-purple to dark brown

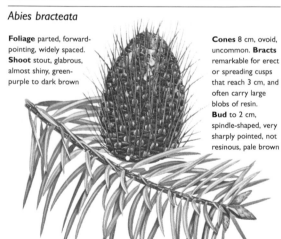

Cones 8 cm, ovoid, uncommon. **Bracts** remarkable for erect or spreading cusps that reach 3 cm, and often carry large blobs of resin.
Bud to 2 cm, spindle-shaped, very sharply pointed, not resinous, pale brown

Leaves to 5 cm, leathery, hard, very sharp spiny tips, persist for up to 5 years, and closely resemble those of California nutmeg (see p 22)

Leaves white-banded below

Unique in its cones, its beech-like buds and its foliage, this silver fir grows wild in the Santa Lucia mountains of California. Manchurian fir (*A. holophylla*) has similar assurgent foliage but ovoid-conic, resinous buds and cylindrical cones with bracts.

Douglas fir • Blue Douglas fir

Pseudotsuga menziesii • Ps. m. ssp. glavea

Douglas foliage densely set, parted above (left), spreads below, emits powerful sweet aroma, can be any shade of green

Leaves to 2.5 cm, with bands below

60 m. Crown columnar

Buds 7 mm, conic, not resinous. **Leaves** have blunt apexes

Blue Douglas foliage (below) set more radially. **Leaves** blue-grey, thick, stand above the shoot in first year, produce little scent. **Apexes** are rounder

Bracts three-pronged, point forwards

Habit slender, grows ragged later. **Foliage** in pendent masses

Blue Douglas cone (right) smaller, 5 cm. **Bracts** sometimes bent back. **Bracts** three-pronged, exserted, spreading or reflexed

Douglas cone (above) 8 cm, green when young

Branches whorled, upswept when young, later heavy, level

Bark smooth, grey when young, later thick, ridged, corky, fissured

The genus *Pseudotsuga* was named after its resemblance to the Hemlocks (pp 58–9) but it also shows an affinity with *Abies* (pp 41–8). Douglas fir, its main species, is native to the western side of the American Rockies and has been widely planted for its vigorous growth and the excellence of its timber. Blue Douglas fir is smaller and slower growing. It differs in its cones and its blunt foliage, and grows wild in the drier eastern Rockies between Montana and Mexico.

True Cedars *Cedrus*

True cedars develop two types of foliage – whorls on short shoots and helical on long shoots, and cones which ripen in the first autumn and slowly disintegrate to scatter the seeds. "Atlas – ascending, Deodar – drooping, Lebanon – level" can be a useful mnemonic.

Cedar of Lebanon

Cedrus libani

40 m. Crown broad, flat-topped. Large, horizontal layers of dense foliage

Bark grey-brown, fissured; smooth, dark grey on young trees

Branches massive, arching then level. **Bole** huge

Foliage dense, darkest green of cedars. Can be grey or glaucous. **Buds** 2–3 mm, brown, ovoid. **Long shoots** brown, pubescent

Cone from 8–14 cm. Apex sometimes depressed. Resinous

Leaves narrow. Taper to sharp, translucent tips. On young, long shoots: 2 cm, set singly and spirally; on older spur-shoots: 3 cm, in short annual whorls of 10–20

Cedar of Lebanon grows naturally in Asia Minor and has become a familiar ornamental in parks and at stately homes. Cyprus cedar (*C. brevifolia*) is less common and has shorter leaves, narrower, more ovoid cones and a more conical crown.

Atlas cedar

Cedrus atlantica

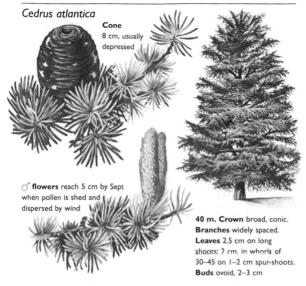

Cone
8 cm, usually
depressed

♂ **flowers** reach 5 cm by Sept
when pollen is shed and
dispersed by wind

40 m. Crown broad, conic.
Branches widely spaced.
Leaves 2.5 cm on long
shoots; 2 cm, in whorls of
30–45 on 1–2 cm spur-shoots.
Buds ovoid, 2–3 cm

Native to the mountains of north Africa, wild Atlas cedars are
found in both green and glaucous forms. The very blue 'Glauca'
clone shown here is the one most commonly encountered as an
ornamental and derives its colour from the wax coating its leaves.

Deodar

Cedrus deodara

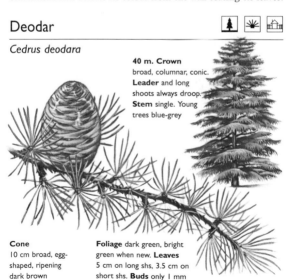

40 m. Crown
broad, columnar, conic.
Leader and long
shoots always droop.
Stem single. Young
trees blue-grey

Cone
10 cm broad, egg-
shaped, ripening
dark brown

Foliage dark green, bright
green when new. **Leaves**
5 cm on long shs, 3.5 cm on
short shs. **Buds** only 1 mm

In the western Himalayas where they grow wild, Deodars can
reach 70 m. Pendulous branchlets on spreading and slightly
downswept branches are their most distinctive features.

51

Larch *Larix*

Some leaves of these deciduous conifers are set singly on long shoots, but most foliage is set in whorls on short spur-like shoots. The small, erect, persistent cones and the short and long shoots are the key identifying features.

European larch • Hybrid larch

Larix decidua • Larix x marschlinsii (syn. L. x eurolepis)

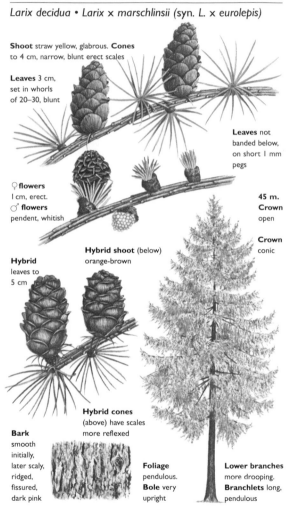

Shoot straw yellow, glabrous. **Cones** to 4 cm, narrow, blunt erect scales

Leaves 3 cm, set in whorls of 20–30, blunt

Leaves not banded below, on short 1 mm pegs

♀ **flowers** 1 cm, erect.
♂ **flowers** pendent, whitish

45 m. Crown open

Crown conic

Hybrid shoot (below) orange-brown

Hybrid leaves to 5 cm

Hybrid cones (above) have scales more reflexed

Bark smooth initially, later scaly, ridged, fissured, dark pink

Foliage pendulous.
Bole very upright

Lower branches more drooping.
Branchlets long, pendulous

Native to the mountains of northern and central Europe, European larch is the only European conifer to shed all its leaves every autumn. Hybrid, or Dunkeld, larch is a natural cross between European and Japanese larch, identifiable by shoots and cones, and is more widely planted for its better form, greater disease resistance and faster growth.

Japanese larch

Larix kaempferi

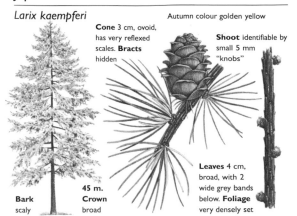

Autumn colour golden yellow

Cone 3 cm, ovoid, has very reflexed scales. **Bracts** hidden

Shoot identifiable by small 5 mm "knobs"

Leaves 4 cm, broad, with 2 wide grey bands below. **Foliage** very densely set

Bark scaly

45 m. Crown broad

This species, native to Mount Fuji, is more vigorous than European larch and forms a shorter, stouter tree with heavier branches. It can be distinguished by its purplish-red shoots, wider leaves and squatter cones with scales reflexed like rose petals.

Tamarack

Larix laricina

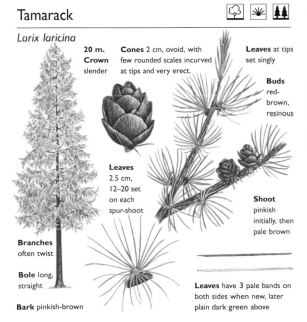

20 m. Crown slender

Cones 2 cm, ovoid, with few rounded scales incurved at tips and very erect.

Leaves at tips set singly

Buds red-brown, resinous

Leaves 2.5 cm, 12–20 set on each spur-shoot

Shoot pinkish initially, then pale brown

Branches often twist

Bole long, straight

Bark pinkish-brown

Leaves have 3 pale bands on both sides when new, later plain dark green above

Tamarack is the most widely distributed conifer in North America growing across Canada from Alaska to the Atlantic, and as far south as Pennsylvania in the USA, in anything from swamps to sub-Arctic conditions. Dahurian larch (*L. gmelinii*) has similar small cones but a gaunt crown and smaller leaves.

53

Spruces *Picea*

Spruces have single pointed needles which are set on a *pulvinus*, a peg-like extension of the shoot. When the needles fall behind this is left making the bare shoots prickly.

Norway spruce

Picea abies

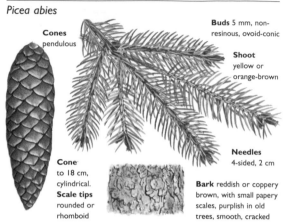

Cones pendulous

Buds 5 mm, non-resinous, ovoid-conic

Shoot yellow or orange-brown

Needles 4-sided, 2 cm

Cone to 18 cm, cylindrical. **Scale tips** rounded or rhomboid

Bark reddish or coppery brown, with small papery scales, purplish in old trees, smooth, cracked

Norway spruce, the familiar "Christmas tree", native to central and northern Europe, has longer needles and longer, less woody cones than Siberian spruce (*P. obovata*), from northern Eurasia, and Wilson spruce (*P. wilsoniana*) which also has ash grey shoots.

Caucasian spruce

Picea orientalis

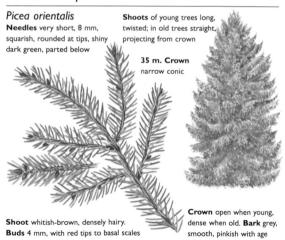

Needles very short, 8 mm, squarish, rounded at tips, shiny dark green, parted below

Shoots of young trees long, twisted; in old trees straight, projecting from crown

35 m. Crown narrow conic

Shoot whitish-brown, densely hairy. **Buds** 4 mm, with red tips to basal scales

Crown open when young, dense when old. **Bark** grey, smooth, pinkish with age

Caucasian spruce is unique in its short needles, and has spindle-shaped, often curved cones that grow to 7 cm. Likiang spruce (*P. likiangensis*) has buff shoots, blue-grey needles and spectacular purple cones to 15 cm with papery scales.

Serbian spruce

Picea omorika

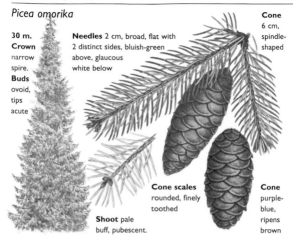

30 m.
Crown narrow spire.
Buds ovoid, tips acute

Needles 2 cm, broad, flat with 2 distinct sides, bluish-green above, glaucous white below

Cone 6 cm, spindle-shaped

Cone scales rounded, finely toothed

Cone purple-blue, ripens brown

Shoot pale buff, pubescent.

Native to a single Balkan river valley but widely planted throughout Europe, this spruce owes its spire like habit not to the branches being short, but to their lying recumbent down the stem before curving out, an adaptation to prevent snow damage.

Sitka spruce

Picea sitchensis

Shoot glabrous, whitish, grooved

Buds ovoid, slightly resinous purple

Scales papery thin, toothed, ripen yellow-brown.
Bark purple-grey, coarse flaking plates in old trees

Cones 8 cm, cylindrical

Leaves 3 cm, bright green with 2 narrow lines above, 2 blue-grey bands below; imbricate above

Sitka spruce is native along the west coast of North America, where it can grow to 80 m. It is widely planted for timber in western Britain. Jezo spruce (*P. jezoensis*), from north-eastern Asia, has denser, assurgent blunt leathery needles to 1.5 cm, and a gaunt habit. Sargent spruce (*P. brachytyla*), from western China, has leaves to 1.5 cm which are silvery white below and curve down at the sides. Its 13 cm cones are conical.

White spruce

Picea glauca

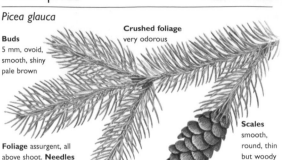

Buds 5 mm, ovoid, smooth, shiny pale brown

Crushed foliage very odorous

Scales smooth, round, thin but woody

Foliage assurgent, all above shoot. **Needles** even length, 1.5 cm, round, grey or blue-grey with narrow white bands

Cone 6 cm, ovoid.

Shoot glabrous, white, later orange-brown

White spruce, which has a wide range across Canada and northern USA, grows to 20 m with a narrow conic crown. Engelmann spruce (*P. engelmannii*) differs in its longer, softer, 2.5 cm needles, hairy shoots and papery scales. Black spruce (*P. mariana*) has 2 cm 4-angled spreading leaves and ovoid cones.

Colorado blue spruce

Picea pungens 'Glauca'

25 m. Crown columnar-conic, dense

Needles 2 cm, arranged radially but upswept below; 4-sided, stiff, sharp

Buds 1 cm, with long slender scales at base

Cone 12 cm, cylindrical. Scales thin, papery. **Margins** wavy

Branches level, later pendent with tips upswept.
Bark thick, purplish-brown, coarse and flaking

This form of the normally grey-green foliage Colorado spruce is the one usually cultivated. Dragon spruce (*P. asperata*) has grey exfoliating papery bark and lacks a ring of scales at the base of the bud; its cones have round woody scales. Tigertail spruce (*P. torano* syn. *P. polita*) has viciously sharp, shiny dark green radial leaves and cones with rounded scales.

Brewer spruce

Picea breweriana

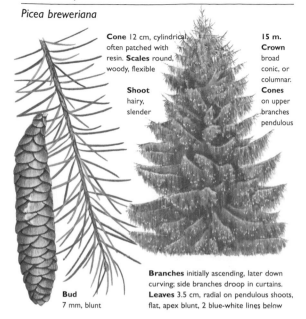

Cone 12 cm, cylindrical, often patched with resin. **Scales** round, woody, flexible

15 m. Crown broad conic, or columnar.

Shoot hairy, slender

Cones on upper branches pendulous

Bud 7 mm, blunt

Branches initially ascending, later down curving; side branches droop in curtains.
Leaves 3.5 cm, radial on pendulous shoots, flat, apex blunt, 2 blue-white lines below

A native of Oregon and California, this fine weeping tree has branchlets drooping vertically either side of the main branches. Sikkim spruce (*P. spinulosa*) has white glabrous shoots on an open, less pendent crown, and its leaves are not so flat.

Morinda spruce

Picea smithiana

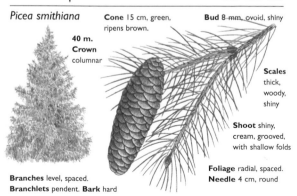

Cone 15 cm, green, ripens brown.

Bud 8 mm, ovoid, shiny

40 m. Crown columnar

Scales thick, woody, shiny

Shoot shiny, cream, grooved, with shallow folds

Foliage radial, spaced.
Needle 4 cm, round

Branches level, spaced.
Branchlets pendent. **Bark** hard

Morinda spruce is native from Afghanistan to Nepal, and has the largest cones of the genus, up to 20 × 5 cm, borne throughout the upper crown. Schrenk spruce (*P. schrenkiana*) from central Asia is similar, but has less weeping branchlets, grey-green leaves less radially arranged and long pale buds.

Hemlocks *Tsuga*

Hemlocks are a small group of conifers differing from spruces in their flattened needles, usually notched at apex, the slender branchlets which lack the prominent *pulvini* of the *Picea* and the cones are less than 3.5 cm.

Western hemlock

Tsuga heterophylla

Needles 2 cm at side but only 1 cm above, tip rounded

50 m. Crown conic, broader on old trees, dense, pendulous tips to straight branches ascending at 45°, low branches droop

Shoots slender, ribbed, cream-brown, hairs brown

Cone 3 cm, pendulous, ovoid, scales rounded, entire

Buds small, ovoid, non-resinous

Young tree (right) has leading shoot which arches over

Leaf has white bands below

Foliage spreading below, parted above

Bark thin, smooth, fissured and ridged in older trees.
Bole straight, fluted; single stem straight from ground to tip of tree

Western hemlock, a native of the western half of North America, is a fast-growing tree with attractive foliage, extremely tolerant of shade and dry, acid conditions. The specific name refers to the irregular foliage arrangement, also a feature of *T. diversifolia*, a Japanese species, which has entire leaf margins, shorter leaves that are vividly white below and orange shoots.

Eastern hemlock

Tsuga canadensis

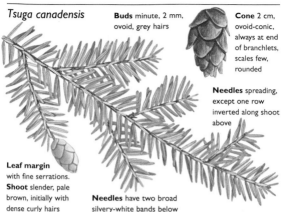

Buds minute, 2 mm, ovoid, grey hairs

Cone 2 cm, ovoid-conic, always at end of branchlets, scales few, rounded

Needles spreading, except one row inverted along shoot above

Leaf margin with fine serrations. **Shoot** slender, pale brown, initially with dense curly hairs

Needles have two broad silvery-white bands below

Unlike *heterophylla*, Eastern hemlock grows on a multiple stem and grows in the eastern half of North America. Carolina hemlock (*T. carolinensis*), from the south-eastern USA, has entire margined needles on shiny orange shoots, and larger long-ovoid cones to 3.5 cm with thin rounded scales.

Mountain hemlock

Hesperopence (Tsuga) mertensiana

Needles 2.5 cm, slender, stomata on both sides

Leaves set all around shoot

Leaves dense, green or grey

Shoot hairy, shiny, pale brown

Bark deeply furrowed with rounded ridges, rough on younger trees and more orangey

30 m. Crown spire-like, tip nodding

Cone 8 cm, cylindrical, tapers at both ends, scales rounded, reflexed when cone open

Mountain hemlock is midway between a *Tsuga* and a *Picea*, differing from Tsuga in the petiole-like base of the needle, the radially set leaves which have stomata on both surfaces and much larger cones with numerous scales. It has a similar though higher distribution to Western hemlock.

Pines *Pinus*

The pines take two summers to ripen their cones (except *P. pinea*, p 62). They can be divided into two main groups – hard pines (e.g. Scots Pine), with hard timber, marked annual growth rings, rough bark and woody cones, and soft pines with softer timber and cones.

Scots pine

Pinus sylvestris

35 m. Crown rounded on old trees, conical when young. **Branches** short, horizontal or slightly ascending

Buds resinous, short-pointed, cylindrical

Cone 8 cm, ovoid, green in 1st year. **Scales** not spined. **Bark** in upper crown orange, flaking, heavily fissured at base

Shoot glabrous, ridged

Leaves 8 cm (15 cm on young trees), broad, stout, twisted, sheath persistent.

This tree has a wide natural range across Europe and Asia from the Atlantic to Pacific. Its change in bark colour and texture is distinctive, as is its grey-green to bright blue-green foliage; that of 'Aurea' is golden in winter. Aleppo pine (*P. halepensis*) has sparser, shiny green leaves, red-brown buds and grey shoots. Its shiny red cones often remain closed on the tree.

Austrian pine • Corsican pine

Pinus nigra var. *nigra* • *P. nigra* var. *maritima*

Austrian: foliage dense, in forward-pointing bunches. **Shoot** ridged and shiny

Leaves 15 cm, stiff, curved in 2nd year. **Sheaths** 1 cm, persistent

Buds long, 12 mm

Bark coarse, deeply furrowed. **Corsican pine** (below): 45 m. **Crown** lighter

Cones (both trees) 8 cm

Corsican: foliage slender, spreading, twisted

Leaves 18 cm, in spaced fascicles. **Bud** resinous

Widely distributed throughout the Mediterranean, Black pine (*P. nigra*) occurs in several forms, two of which are shown here: Austrian pine is a hardy, densely crowned tree, usually growing on several stems to 30 m, Corsican pine is more vigorous and often planted for its timber. Their cones are identical but they can usually be identified by their shoots, buds and leaves. bosnian pine (*P. heldreichii* var. *leucodermis*) has similarly dense foliage but cobalt blue unripe cones and bloomed shoots.

Shore pine • Lodgepole pine

Pinus contorta var. *contorta* • *P. contorta* var. *latifolia*

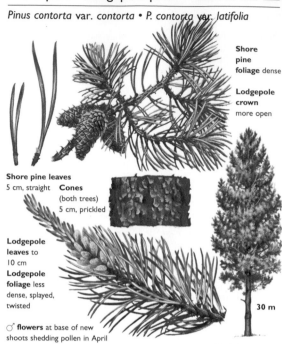

Shore pine foliage dense

Lodgepole crown more open

Shore pine leaves 5 cm, straight

Cones (both trees) 5 cm, prickled

Lodgepole leaves to 10 cm

Lodgepole foliage less dense, splayed, twisted

♂ **flowers** at base of new shoots shedding pollen in April

30 m

Bark finely scaled

Extensively planted in European forests, these trees can be distinguished by their foliage. Jack pine (*P. banksiana*) has shorter, 4 cm leaves and curved, forward-pointing cones.

Stone pine

Pinus pinea

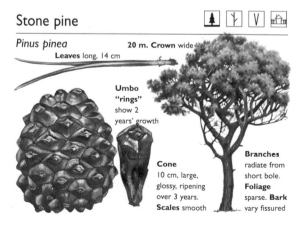

Leaves long, 14 cm

20 m. Crown wide

Umbo "rings" show 2 years' growth

Cone 10 cm, large, glossy, ripening over 3 years. **Scales** smooth

Branches radiate from short bole. **Foliage** sparse. **Bark** vary fissured

Instantly recognizable by its umbrella-shaped crown, this Mediterranean species has large, 2 cm, wingless seeds which have been a culinary delicacy since the time of the Romans.

Maritime pine

Pinus pinaster

Umbos upcurved

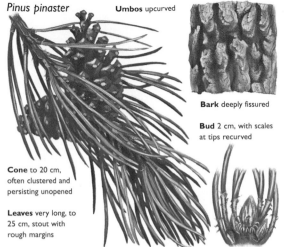

Bark deeply fissured

Bud 2 cm, with scales at tips recurved

Cone to 20 cm, often clustered and persisting unopened

Leaves very long, to 25 cm, stout with rough margins

This tree thrives on poor, sandy sites and is widely planted in Mediterranean countries for its resin. This is tapped by longitudinal wounds made in the bark and is used in turpentine manufacture. Its leaves are the longest and stoutest of any European pine.

Monterey pine

Pinus radiata

Leaves long, 15 cm, slender, soft, shiny

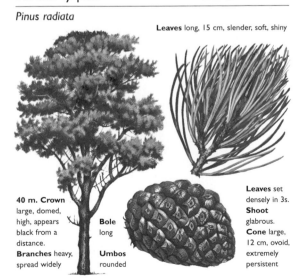

40 m. Crown large, domed, high, appears black from a distance.
Branches heavy, spread widely

Bole long

Umbos rounded

Leaves set densely in 3s.
Shoot glabrous.
Cone large, 12 cm, ovoid, extremely persistent

Native to California, this tree has been widely planted for its timber. Its obliquely based cones may persist for over twenty years and often require the heat of forest fires to open them.

Ponderosa pine

Pinus ponderosa

**40 m.
Crown** variable

Crown fairly open.
Bole long, straight

Leaves 15–25 cm

Leaves dense, stout, usually in fascicles of 3.
Sheath 2 cm, persistent

Cone 12 cm, when falls base left behind.
Scales ridged, prickled

This tree grows at varying altitudes and on dry sites throughout western North America. Its foliage is very variable – even on the same tree. Leaves may be set in fascicles of both two and three.

Jeffrey pine

Pinus jeffreyi

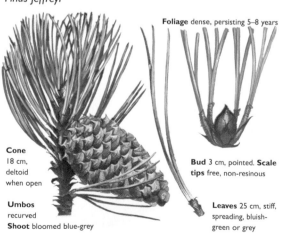

Foliage dense, persisting 5–8 years

Cone 18 cm, deltoid when open

Umbos recurved
Shoot bloomed blue-grey

Bud 3 cm, pointed. **Scale tips** free, non-resinous

Leaves 25 cm, stiff, spreading, bluish-green or grey

Native to Oregon and California and rarely exceeding 35 m, Jeffrey pine is smaller than Ponderosa but can grow at greater heights. Its distinguishing features are its bloomed shoot, and when available, its larger, broad-based cones.

Coulter pine

Pinus coulterii

Cone huge, 35 cm, weighs up to 2.5 kg. **Seeds** 12 mm. **Scales** thick. **Umbos** sharp

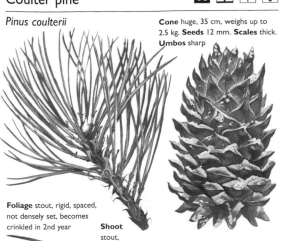

Foliage stout, rigid, spaced, not densely set, becomes crinkled in 2nd year

Shoot stout, glabrous

Leaves 30 cm. **Sheath** 2.5 cm

While closely related to Ponderosa and Jeffrey pines, Coulter pine can be recognized by the size of its cones, normally set at the summit, or its longer hanging leaves. Digger pine (*P. sabiniana*) holds its 25 cm leaves level.

Lacebark pine

Pinus bungeana

Foliage spaced, not set densely on shoot

Bark smooth, flaking through white, yellow, olive and purple to grey-green

Leaves 8 cm, slender, smooth, finely toothed, in close fascicles

Sheath deciduous

Cone 6 cm, on 2 cm stalk. **Umbos** dorsal, spined

This species has a low, usually bushy crown and is cultivated for the splendour of its bark. This is initially smooth and grey-green and then flakes away to leave rounded white patches which turn through yellow, green, red and purple to purple-brown. In its native China, the bark of old trees turns a further chalk white.

Arolla pine

Pinus cembra

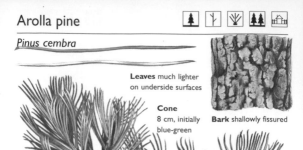

Leaves much lighter on underside surfaces

Cone 8 cm, initially blue-green

Bark shallowly fissured

Leaves 10 cm, finely toothed, triangular in section, set closely

Shoot has dense rufous hairs

Arolla, or Swiss stone pine, grows wild at high altitudes in the mountains of central Europe, while in parts of Scandinavia it is planted for its timber. Its contrasting leaves and broad, dense crown reaching 25 m are distinctive. The large seeds are edible.

Macedonian pine

Pinus peyce

30 m

Crown dense

Leaves 12 cm, dense

Leaves dense, rigid

Umbos incurved

Branches whorled, very upswept in upper crown

Cone 15 cm, stalked. **Scales** thin, convex

Rarely planted for timber outside its native range in the Balkans, this attractive tree is similar to Blue pine but has finer shoots, more curved cones and leaves which are shorter, denser, rigid and more forward-pointing.

Blue pine

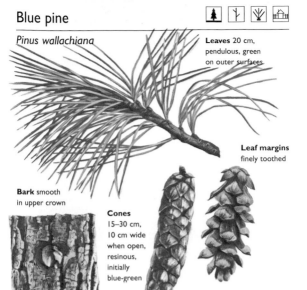

Pinus wallachiana

Leaves 20 cm, pendulous, green on outer surfaces

Leaf margins finely toothed

Bark smooth in upper crown

Cones 15–30 cm, 10 cm wide when open, resinous, initially blue-green

Scales incurved except at base. **Cone stalk** 4 cm

Blue pine, (syn. *P. excelsa*), is indigenous throughout the Himalayas. It has been widely planted as an ornamental and forms a broad, heavily branched tree to 35 m, with stout, glabrous shoots and curved leaves. Mexican white pine (*P. ayacahuite*) has straight needles and more tapered cones.

Armand pine

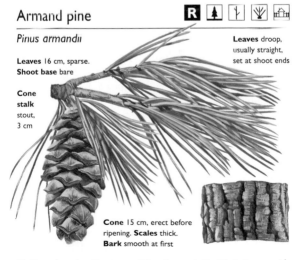

Pinus armandii

Leaves droop, usually straight, set at shoot ends

Leaves 16 cm, sparse. **Shoot base** bare

Cone stalk stout, 3 cm

Cone 15 cm, erect before ripening. **Scales** thick. **Bark** smooth at first

Dedicated to its discoverer, Père Armand David, it has a wide distribution across China and in Burma. It resembles Blue pine but has finer shoots and barrel-shaped cones with 1.5 cm seeds.

Japanese white pine

Pinus parviflora

Foliage
blue-green on
outer surface,
silvery glaucous
on inner

Leaves
5–8 cm,
slender,
twisted,
blunt, set
together in
1st year,
splaying
out later.
Margins
very finely
toothed.
Sheath
1 cm,
deciduous

Cones 5 cm,
egg-shaped,
almost sessile

Umbos
slender
and terminal.
Seeds 1 cm

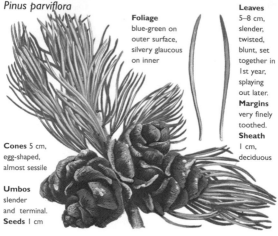

In its wild form, this species grows to a height of 25 m but is more usually encountered as a lower, slow-growing tree that rarely reaches 10 m. It has a wide crown and tiered branches and was probably developed for Japanese ornamental gardens. The leaves of both types are the most twisting of any pine.

Western white pine

Pinus monticola

Foliage dense,
set in tufts

Cones 35 cm, tapering, slightly curved,
set on short stalks, numerous. **Scales**
thin, rounded, resinous

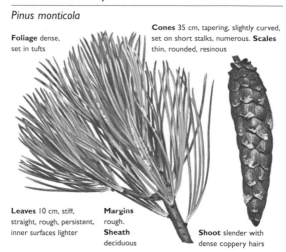

Leaves 10 cm, stiff,
straight, rough, persistent,
inner surfaces lighter

Margins
rough.
Sheath
deciduous

Shoot slender with
dense coppery hairs

Native to the Pacific coast of North America and as far inland as Montana. *P. monticola* has a dense crown and can reach heights of 50 m. Like all soft pines, the bark of young trees and that high up on old trees is smooth and grey-green. It is often attacked by blister rust, a fungal disease which affects all American white pines and kills many old trees.

Weymouth pine

Pinus strobus

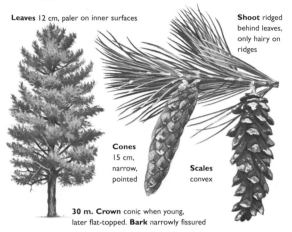

Leaves 12 cm, paler on inner surfaces

Shoot ridged behind leaves, only hairy on ridges

Cones 15 cm, narrow, pointed

Scales convex

30 m. Crown conic when young, later flat-topped. **Bark** narrowly fissured

Native to the forests of eastern North America, Weymouth pine forms a tree to 40 m, often on several stems, and differs from Western white pine in its glabrous shoots and shorter, pointed cones which are only 15 cm high. The leaves are stiffer and only persist for two seasons. It is susceptible to white pine blister rust.

Bristlecone pine

Pinus aristata

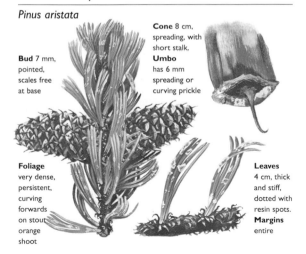

Bud 7 mm, pointed, scales free at base

Cone 8 cm, spreading, with short stalk.
Umbo has 6 mm spreading or curving prickle

Foliage very dense, persistent, curving forwards on stout orange shoot

Leaves 4 cm, thick and stiff, dotted with resin spots.
Margins entire

The most common of the species from south-western USA which are known as "foxtail" pines because of their long, dense foliage, Bristlecone pine has leaves which persist for up to 15 years. Balfour pine (*P. balfouriana*) survives at high altitudes and has longer, unspotted leaves and cones with less prominent spines.

The broadleaf trees

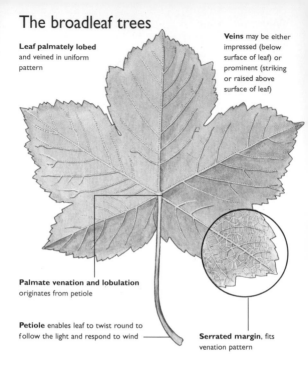

Leaf palmately lobed and veined in uniform pattern

Veins may be either impressed (below surface of leaf) or prominent (striking or raised above surface of leaf)

Palmate venation and lobulation originates from petiole

Petiole enables leaf to twist round to follow the light and respond to wind

Serrated margin, fits venation pattern

The trees known as the broadleaf trees, because their leaves have broad blades, are more properly classified as the Angiospermae, so called because their seeds develop from ovules which are enclosed in an ovary. All but two can also be classified as Dicotyledonae, because their seedlings have two seed leaves. They are also called hardwoods, as they produce hard timber.

The shape of the leaf is the best feature for identification purposes, and is governed by its composition and function, a vital element being the venation system, illustrated above in a sycamore leaf. The veins strengthen the thin blade, and the many complex patterns they form are useful for identification. Their main function is to move the products of photosynthesis around the plant. Photosynthesis has to take place in daylight and needs water, which is transported up from the root system to spread across the surface of the leaf blade through the network of veins. The veins are two-way channels: they transport water and nutrients to the leaf, and carry the sugar sap, the end product of photosynthesis, to the rest of the tree.

Most water from the roots, however, transpires or evaporates into the atmosphere, something which happens to a far lesser extent in most conifers because the thick waxy surface of their thin needles retains moisture. Temperate broadleaf trees are nearly all deciduous, dropping all their leaves each winter. Once the temperature drops, the tree cannot extract from the cold soil enough water to maintain transpiration, and freezing temperatures would damage the leaves. The nutrient material is withdrawn from the leaves before they wither and die, and they then fall, leaving a scar behind where they grew from the shoot. The leaves decay on the ground to form a rich mould.

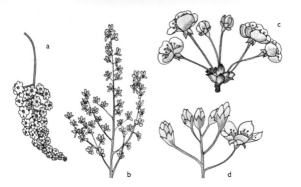

Flowers

The broadleaf trees flower for a relatively short time, but these flowers are very useful in identification. While conifers transfer the pollen from the male to the female flowers on the wind, most broadleaves are insect pollinated, and their flowers have brightly coloured petals and strong scents to attract the insects. Four types of flower arrangement are illustrated above. A **raceme (a)** is a simple groups of stalked flowers on a long single rachis. A **panicle (b)** is a looser compound or branched flower cluster. An **umbel (c)** is an inflorescence with pedicels all rising from the same point. A **corymb (d)** is a flat-topped flower cluster in which the outside flowers open first.

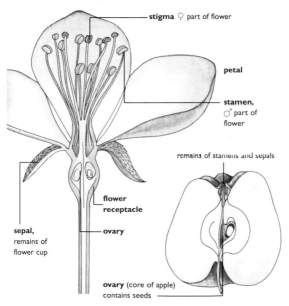

One mode of the transition from flower to fruit is illustrated with the apple above. In apples the flesh develops from the flower receptacle, and once the petals have dropped, the stamens and sepals wither until their remains are at the base of the fruit. What was the ovary becomes the core of the apple, which contains the seeds.

Fruit

The basic function of the fruit is to protect the seeds as they develop and to assist in their dispersal to propagate the species. The fruit may be sparser than the flowers, either because some of the flowers did not develop or because the majority of the inflorescence was male. There are several different types of fruit: the apple illustrated on the previous page is a **pome,** which has a fleshy covering around one or more seeds in several fused cells; some other examples are illustrated below. A **capsule (a),** as borne by eucalyptus trees, is a hard woody pod which releases many small seeds through 3–6 terminal pores. A **drupe (b),** such as a cherry has a fleshy exterior around a stone which contains one or more seeds. A **cone-like structure (c),** as borne by the alders, has spirally or oppositely arranged scales which each carry two or more seeds. A **samara (d),** as borne by ashes, has a single seed in a case on the end of a long wing. A **nut (e),** such as the acorn, bears its seeds inside a hard shell; the acorn is set in a cup called an **involucre** or **cupule.**

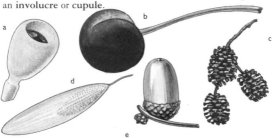

Seed germination

The few seeds which alight on suitable ground can lie dormant for one or two years before germination. They are gradually softened by moisture from the soil, and eventually a tiny root is produced by cell division, which breaks through the seed coat and penetrates the ground. It next develops tiny hairs to extract water and nutrients from the earth; these are renewed every year throughout its life. sometimes two seed leaves withdraw from the withered seed casing as the seedling, the first plant, is formed. In the Horse chestnut, illustrated below, they remain inside.

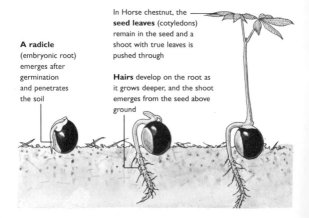

In Horse chestnut, the **seed leaves** (cotyledons) remain in the seed and a shoot with true leaves is pushed through

A radicle (embryonic root) emerges after germination and penetrates the soil

Hairs develop on the root as it grows deeper, and the shoot emerges from the seed above ground

Willow family *Salicaceae*

This family has 350 or so species of willow and poplar which are mainly natives of the northern hemisphere. The chief feature uniting them all is their flowers. These have neither petals nor sepals and are borne in catkins which usually appear with or before their tree's new leaves and are either male or female. Only one type is usually carried. The seeds are very small but fluffy with white cottony down which assists dispersal. Both willows and poplars prefer moist sites and hybridize so easily that positive identification is not always easy.

Poplars *Populus*

Poplars have wind-pollinated catkins and leaves whose broad blades have long petioles which may be flattened at one end. Their shoots bear terminal buds and all their buds have overlapping scales.

White poplar, Abele

Populus alba

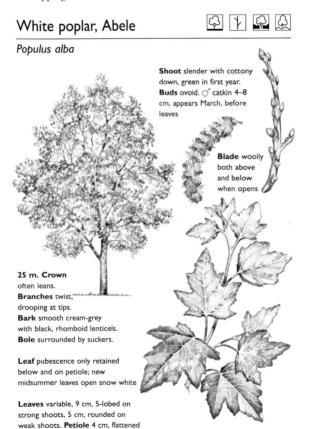

Shoot slender with cottony down, green in first year.
Buds ovoid. ♂ catkin 4–8 cm, appears March, before leaves

Blade woolly both above and below when opens

25 m. Crown often leans.
Branches twist, drooping at tips.
Bark smooth cream-grey with black, rhomboid lenticels.
Bole surrounded by suckers.

Leaf pubescence only retained below and on petiole; new midsummer leaves open snow white

Leaves variable, 9 cm, 5-lobed on strong shoots, 5 cm, rounded on weak shoots. **Petiole** 4 cm, flattened

White poplar is native to central and southern Europe, North Africa and central Asia and, with Aspen (p 74), belongs to a group of poplars with smooth barks and lobed or coarsely serrate leaves. 'Pyramidalis' is a fastigiate clone, broader than Lombardy poplar (p 75); 'Richardii' has golden yellow leaves.

Grey poplar

Populus x canescens

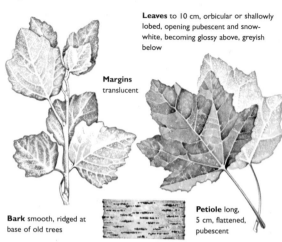

Leaves to 10 cm, orbicular or shallowly lobed, opening pubescent and snow-white, becoming glossy above, greyish below

Margins translucent

Bark smooth, ridged at base of old trees

Petiole long, 5 cm, flattened, pubescent

This natural hybrid of White poplar (p 73) and Aspen reaches a height of some 35 m on a few large and heavy, arching branches. Its leaves are closer to those of the former species but their undersides are greyer and less downy; they differ from those of Aspen in being persistently pubescent below. Female Grey poplars are rare and suckering is the usual form of regeneration.

Aspen

Populus tremula

Leaves usually downy and coppery when opening; soon glabrous and green, turning yellow or gold in autumn

Shoot shiny, hairless

Petiole 6 cm, thin and very flattened, flexible near blade

20 m. Crown open, lightly branched. **Bark** smooth but ridged, greyish at base of older trees

Teeth shallow, blunt, irregular. **Margins** sinuous, translucent

With a natural range extending across the Eurasian landmass, this hardy species grows equally well on exposed high ground or wet lowland where its practice of suckering profusely helps to colonize and consolidate the soil. Aspen's distinctive petiole allows the slightest breeze to flutter the leaves.

Black poplars

Populus nigra

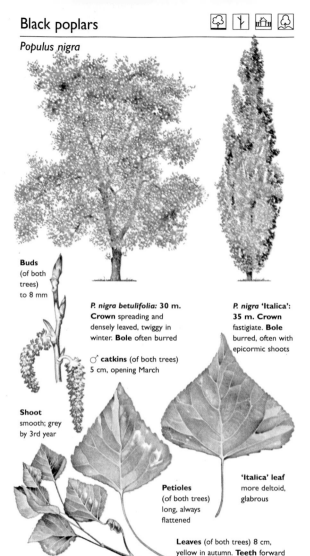

Buds
(of both trees) to 8 mm

P. nigra betulifolia: 30 m.
Crown spreading and densely leaved, twiggy in winter. **Bole** often burred

♂ **catkins** (of both trees) 5 cm, opening March

P. nigra 'Italica':
35 m. Crown fastigiate. **Bole** burred, often with epicormic shoots

Shoot
smooth; grey by 3rd year

Petioles
(of both trees) long, always flattened

'Italica' leaf
more deltoid, glabrous

Leaves (of both trees) 8 cm, yellow in autumn. **Teeth** forward curved. **Margins** thick, translucent

The black poplar normally encountered in Britain is *P. nigra* var. *betulifolia* and differs from its rarer continental type (*P. nigra*) in having birch-like leaves and initially downy twigs and leaf stalks. Its burred bole is diagnostic. The more common Lombardy poplar (*P. n.* 'Italica') may have arisen in central Asia rather than northern Italy as its name implies. the similar 'Plantierensis' clone has a leafier, slightly broader crown and initially pubescent petioles and shoots, nearly glabrous by midsummer. *Pemphigus bursarinus* aphids often attack these poplars and produce distinctively spiralled galls on their leaf stalks.

Hybrid black poplars

Populus x *euramericana*

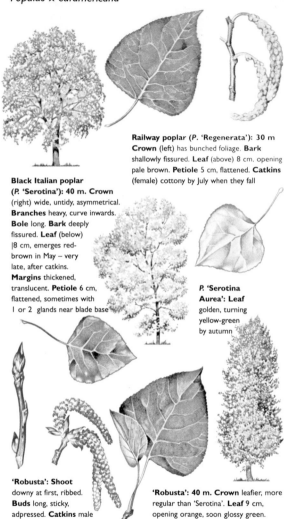

Railway poplar (*P.* 'Regenerata'): 30 m
Crown (left) has bunched foliage. **Bark**
shallowly fissured. **Leaf** (above) 8 cm, opening
pale brown. **Petiole** 5 cm, flattened. **Catkins**
(female) cottony by July when they fall

Black Italian poplar
(*P.* 'Serotina'): 40 m. **Crown**
(right) wide, untidy, asymmetrical.
Branches heavy, curve inwards.
Bole long. **Bark** deeply
fissured. **Leaf** (below)
|8 cm, emerges red-
brown in May – very
late, after catkins.
Margins thickened,
translucent. **Petiole** 6 cm,
flattened, sometimes with
1 or 2 glands near blade base

**P. 'Serotina
Aurea'**: **Leaf**
golden, turning
yellow-green
by autumn

'Robusta': **Shoot**
downy at first, ribbed.
Buds long, sticky,
adpressed. **Catkins** male
numerous in April

'Robusta': 40 m. **Crown** leafier, more
regular than 'Serotina'. **Leaf** 9 cm,
opening orange, soon glossy green.
Petiole 9 cm, minutely downy.

Hybrid black poplars have been developed from vegetative
cuttings taken from crossings of *Populus nigra* (p 75) and the
closely related American cottonwood (*P. deltoides*). As clones they
are either male or female trees and while technically cultivars of
P. x *euramericana*, are more usually known by their varietal
names. Of the hybrids shown here, 'Regenerata' is the only female,
'Serotina' the most widespread and 'Robusta' the fastest growing.
Their hybrid vigour, clean, unburred boles and a resistance to
disease make such black poplars important for their timber.

Balsam poplars

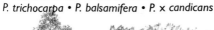

P. trichocarpa • *P. balsamifera* • *P.* x *candicans*

Western balsam: ♂ catkin (right) long and thick, 8 × 1.5 cm, appearing in April before leaves. **Buds** 2 cm, appressed, resinous, slightly pubescent. **Fruit** (above) 3-valved, hairy, cottony by May when it is shed

Western balsam (*P. trichocarpa*): 35 m. Crown conic. **Branches** whorled, numerous. **Leaves** (right) large, 15–30 cm, thick, yellow in autumn, always yellowish-white below. **Petioles** 3 cm, stout round

Eastern balsam (*P. balsamifera*): **Shoot** (right) round, not angled. **Bud** longer than those of Western balsam, adpressed. **Leaves** (below) 12 cm, broader, more obtuse than Western balsam but very variable. **Blades** glabrous, slightly downy below, finely serrate. **Petioles** 7 cm, round

Balm of Gilead poplar (*P.* x *candicans*): **Leaves** (above) 15 cm, downy beneath. **Margins** ciliate. **Petioles** 7 cm, downy, roundish. **Shoot** hairy initially, angular. **'Aurora' summer leaves** (top) develop cream-white and pink marbling

These trees are recognizable by the balsamiferous odour pervaded by their large, resinous buds and new foliage in early summer. Their leaves are always yellow-white below and have neither flattened leaf stalks nor translucent margins. Western and Eastern balsams are both native to North America and are fast-growing, the latter putting out suckers around its bole. Balm of Gilead poplar produces these so easily and profusely that they soon become a nuisance, and since its trunk is also prone to bacterial canker, its planting is not recommended; the 'Aurora' form, with variegated foliage, is preferable. The Chinese balsam poplar (*P. szechuanica*) is notable for its very large leaves whose undersides are initially downy and purple.

Berlin poplar

Populus × *berolinensis*

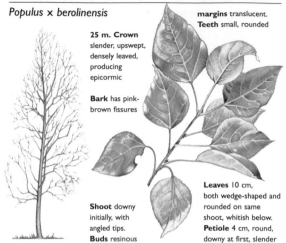

25 m. Crown slender, upswept, densely leaved, producing epicormic

Bark has pink-brown fissures

margins translucent. **Teeth** small, rounded

Shoot downy initially, with angled tips. **Buds** resinous

Leaves 10 cm, both wedge-shaped and rounded on same shoot, whitish below. **Petiole** 4 cm, round, downy at first, slender

A cross between Lombardy poplar (p 75) and Siberian poplar (*P. laurifolia*), from which it derives its rhomboid leaves, this tree is well adapted to severe climatic extremes and is widely planted in continental Europe. Simon poplar (*P. simonii*), from China, has shorter leaf stalks, obovate leaves and whitish bark.

Necklace poplar

Populus lasiocarpa

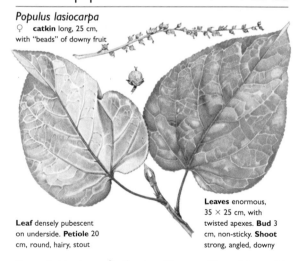

♀ **catkin** long, 25 cm, with "beads" of downy fruit

Leaf densely pubescent on underside. **Petiole** 20 cm, round, hairy, stout

Leaves enormous, 35 × 25 cm, with twisted apexes. **Bud** 3 cm, non-sticky. **Shoot** strong, angled, downy

Recognizable at once by the size of its magnificent foliage, this tree is native to moist woodland sites in western China. Its closest relative, *P. wilsoniana*, from the same area, has smaller, sea-green leaves which are not pubescent on their undersides, flattened leaf stalks and buds which are resinous.

Willows *Salix*

Unlike poplars, willows are insect-pollinated, having stiffer, nectar-bearing catkins as well as longer and narrower stipulate leaves, shorter petioles and single-scaled buds. Their shoots lack terminal buds and growth occurs laterally behind the tips.

White willow • Silver willow

Salix alba • *S. alba* 'Sericea'

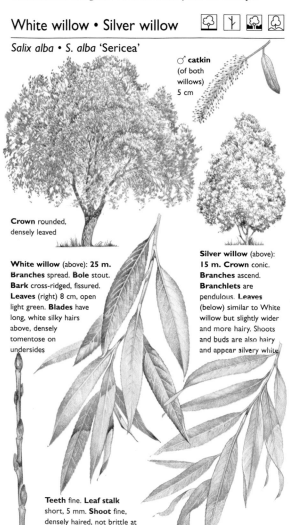

♂ **catkin** (of both willows) 5 cm

Crown rounded, densely leaved

White willow (above): 25 m. Branches spread. **Bole** stout. **Bark** cross-ridged, fissured. **Leaves** (right) 8 cm, open light green. **Blades** have long, white silky hairs above, densely tomentose on undersides

Silver willow (above): 15 m. **Crown** conic. **Branches** ascend. **Branchlets** are pendulous. **Leaves** (below) similar to White willow but slightly wider and more hairy. Shoots and buds are also hairy and appear silvery white

Teeth fine. **Leaf stalk** short, 5 mm. **Shoot** fine, densely haired, not brittle at base. **Buds** 2 mm, flattened

Native to most of Europe, this vigorous species is one of the tallest willows and while sometimes confused with Crack willow (p 80), can be distinguished by its far less fragile twigs and its less deeply fissured bark. It is often pollarded to produce pliant shoots which are used for basketry. The widely distributed 'Sericea' is readily identified by its colouring and more hairy foliage.

Coral-bark willow

Salix alba 'Chermesina'

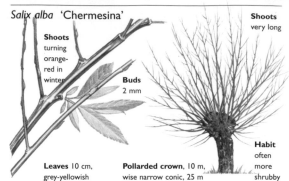

Shoots
very long

Shoots
turning
oranged-
red in
winter

Buds
2 mm

Habit
often
more
shrubby

Leaves 10 cm,
grey-yellowish

Pollarded crown, 10 m,
wise narrow conic, 25 m

Because it is often pruned back heavily to encourage the growth of its long, colourful shoots, this willow seldom reaches its potential height. It is one of several scarlet forms.

Cricket-bat willow

Salix 'Cœrulea'

Leaves
initially
hairy

Shoot slender,
purplish
Leaves broader, less
hairy than White willow

This vigorous, female tree is probably a hybrid of *S. alba* and *S. fragilis* and its light, resilient wood is ideal for cricket bats.

Crack willow

Salix fragilis

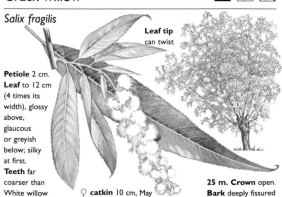

Leaf tip
can twist

Petiole 2 cm.
Leaf to 12 cm
(4 times its
width), glossy
above,
glaucous
or greyish
below; silky
at first.
Teeth far
coarser than
White willow

♀ **catkin** 10 cm, May

25 m. Crown open.
Bark deeply fissured

Very similar to *S. alba* and also grown in pollarded form on moist sites, this willow can be distinguished by its larger, more coarsely toothed leaves. Its brittle twigs give the tree its name.

Weeping willow

Salix x sepulcralis 'Chyrsocuma'

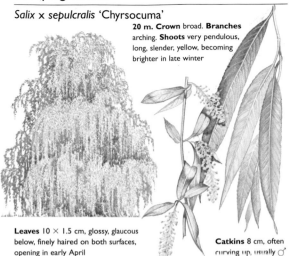

20 m. Crown broad. **Branches** arching. **Shoots** very pendulous, long, slender, yellow, becoming brighter in late winter

Leaves 10 × 1.5 cm, glossy, glaucous below, finely haired on both surfaces, opening in early April

Catkins 8 cm, often curving up, usually ♂

Attractive beside water towards which its foliage tends to bend, this is a hybrid of White willow and Chinese weeping willow (*S. babylonica*) which is far less common and has pendulous *brown* shoots and leaves with fewer teeth.

Corkscrew willow

Salix matsudana 'Tortuosa'

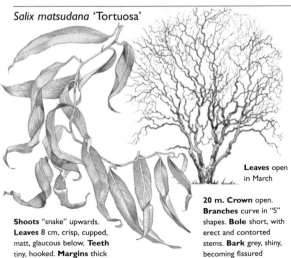

Leaves open in March

20 m. Crown open. **Branches** curve in "S" shapes. **Bole** short, with erect and contorted stems. **Bark** grey, shiny, becoming fissured

Shoots "snake" upwards. **Leaves** 8 cm, crisp, cupped, matt, glaucous below. **Teeth** tiny, hooked. **Margins** thick

Useful on dry soils, this makes an attractive garden tree. Its leaves are among the first to appear and the last to fall; in winter its distinctively contorted crown, which can only be confused with that of the Corkscrew hazel, is seen to particularly good effect.

Salix cinerea • *Salix caprea*

Grey willow leaves 8 cm **Veins** impressed, hairy below. **Stipules** persist

Grey willow (above): **10 m. Crown** rounded on several stems but variable, can be shrubby

Sallow (right) **10 m. Crown** open. **Bole** often sinuous

Sallow leaves to 10 cm, usually obovate but variable, finely pubescent below

Sallow catkins (♂ and ♀) silky in late winter

Buds 4 mm, red

Petiole dark red

Shoot initially grey with long hairs, but shiny, glabrous, red-brown by winter; unlike Grey willow, not ridged in 2nd year when bark removed

♂ flower (above) 3 cm, opens Mar, before lvs

♀ catkins (right) 5 cm, green when in flower, release fluffy white seeds in May

Grey willow and Goat or Common Sallow belong to a group of intricately related species which are collectively known as Pussy willows. These are most attractive when their catkins begin to expand in late winter and early spring and are the flowering shoots used to decorate churches on Palm Sunday. The willows illustrated here have similar catkins but the shoot of *S. cinerea* remains densely pubescent; its leaves often have rust coloured hairs below, especially in the subspecies *atrocinerea*, which tends to have less downy shoots and is more treelike. All Pussy willows require damp soil for their seeds to germinate.

Osier

Salix viminalis

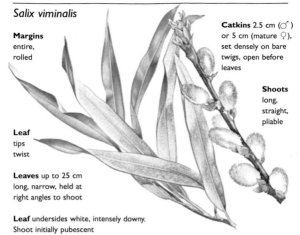

Margins
entire,
rolled

Catkins 2.5 cm (♂)
or 5 cm (mature ♀),
set densely on bare
twigs, open before
leaves

Shoots
long,
straight,
pliable

Leaf
tips
twist

Leaves up to 25 cm
long, narrow, held at
right angles to shoot

Leaf undersides white, intensely downy.
Shoot initially pubescent

Osier has a wide range both throughout Europe and in Asia as far east as the Himalayas and Siberia. Growing to 10 m as a tree, it is found beside rivers and on other wet sites, where it is grown to produce the flexible wands used in basket-making, the trees being coppiced annually for this. Hoary willow (*S. elaeagnos*) has more slender, feathery leaves up to 15 cm long and curved catkins.

Bay willow

Salix pentandra

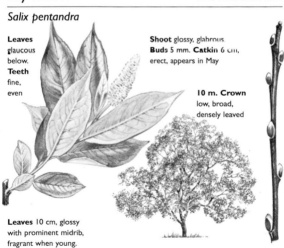

Leaves
glaucous
below.
Teeth
fine,
even

Shoot glossy, glabrous.
Buds 5 mm. **Catkin** 6 cm,
erect, appears in May

10 m. Crown
low, broad,
densely leaved

Leaves 10 cm, glossy
with prominent midrib,
fragrant when young.
Petiole 8 mm

Notable for its dark, glossy leaves and the lateness of its flowers which appear in late May, this grows throughout europe and western Asia. Violet willow (*S. daphnoides*) has white lanceolate leaves, male catkins and a purplish bloom on its winter twigs.

Walnut family *Juglandaceae*

This is a group of large trees with pinnate leaves and male catkins which hang on the tree through winter. The fruit, usually edible, is a drupe or nut and in *Juglans* and *Pterocarya* the pith is chambered.

Walnut

Juglans regia

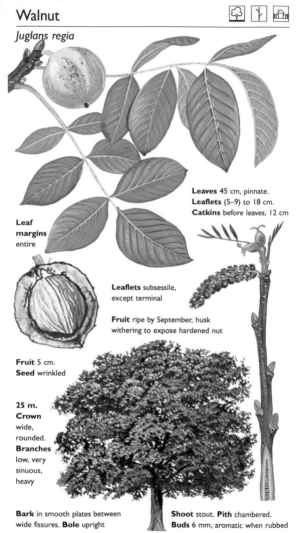

Leaves 45 cm, pinnate.
Leaflets (5–9) to 18 cm.
Catkins before leaves, 12 cm

Leaf margins entire

Leaflets subsessile, except terminal

Fruit ripe by September, husk withering to expose hardened nut

Fruit 5 cm.
Seed wrinkled

25 m.
Crown wide, rounded.
Branches low, very sinuous, heavy

Bark in smooth plates between wide fissures. **Bole** upright

Shoot stout. **Pith** chambered.
Buds 6 mm, aromatic when rubbed

Walnut has become widely naturalized throughout Europe and across Asia and been cultivated since the earliest times, although its exact origin is unknown. Large orchards of it exist in France and California. The fruit is either picked for pickling before the end of July while still fleshy or left until autumn when the nut has hardened. *J. regia* is the only walnut with entire leaflets.

Black walnut

Juglans nigra

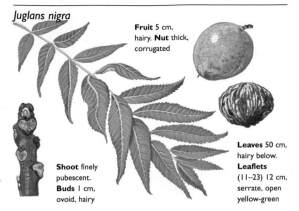

Fruit 5 cm, hairy. **Nut** thick, corrugated

Shoot finely pubescent. **Buds** 1 cm, ovoid, hairy

Leaves 50 cm, hairy below. **Leaflets** (11–23) 12 cm, serrate, open yellow-green

This North American tree has a dark, cross-furrowed bark and a crown which can reach 30 m and is narrower than that of Walnut. Its larger leaves usually have more leaflets. Butternut (*J. cinerea*) has larger leaves, to 80 cm, and sticky, hairy fruit.

Wingnut

Pterocarya fraxinifolia

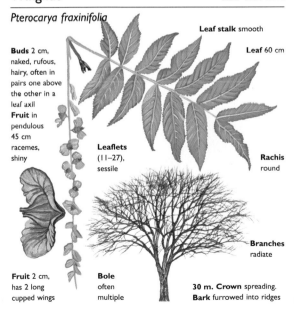

Leaf stalk smooth

Leaf 60 cm

Buds 2 cm, naked, rufous, hairy, often in pairs one above the other in a leaf axil
Fruit in pendulous 45 cm racemes, shiny

Leaflets (11–27), sessile

Rachis round

Branches radiate

Fruit 2 cm, has 2 long cupped wings

Bole often multiple

30 m. Crown spreading. **Bark** furrowed into ridges

This vigorous tree from western Asia is usually surrounded by suckers and has twigs with chambered piths. It is easily recognized by its naked buds and hanging seed catkins. Rehder wingnut (*P.* x *rehderiana*) has flanged leaf stalks.

Bitternut

Carya cordiformis

Leaflets serrate

25 m. Crown more open in older trees

Branches slender.
Bark grey, fissured

Shoot
slender with white lenticels.
Buds to 2.5 cm, slender, yellow, pubescent

Leaves 25 cm.
Fruit 4 cm, encloses 4-ribbed nut

A species with a wide natural range throughout the eastern USA, this hickory grows to 20 m and is identifiable by the taste of its seeds and its yellow winter buds. Its leaves have up to 11 leaflets that are paler below and turn yellow in autumn. Pignut (*C. glabra*) has unribbed seeds and leaves with 5 glabrous leaflets.

Shagbark hickory

Carya ovata

Bark has long vertical plates peeling at ends, smooth when young

Leaves to 65 cm.
Leaflets to 30 cm; terminal on stout, 4 cm petiole

Fruit 5 cm, with 4-lobed husk, set in 2s or 3s on stout pedicel. **Nut** smooth, 4-ribbed, sweet

Leaflets usually in 5s, thick, hard, oily

Rachis stout

This species is instantly identifiable by the nature of its bark which begins to flake into long, curling plates when the tree is about 25 years old. Shellbark hickory (*C. laciniosa*) has similar mature bark but its leaves have 7 leaflets with downy undersides.

Birch family *Betulaceae*

A group of trees and shrubs comprising over 40 species, the members of this family carry separate male and female catkins on the same tree, the females being small, initially erect when flowering, and held above the males. In *Betula* (pp 87–9), *Alnus* (pp 90–1) and *Corylus* (p 92), the males develop in autumn and are carried exposed over winter, opening to release their pollen before, or when, the leaves appear in spring. Those of *Carpinus* (p 93), although pre-formed, are hidden in the winter buds.

Silver birch

Betula pendula

Leaves 7 cm, doubly serrate

Leaves roughish, glabrous below

♂ catkin 3 cm, opens March–April, **♀ catkin** (right) 3 cm, ripens brown

Bole fluted

Buds 4 mm. **Shoot** warty

30 m. Crown narrow. **Branches** ascend when young, later very pendulous. **Bark** smooth, red-brown on young trees

'Dalecarlica': **Leaves** 5 cm. **Margins** deeply dissected. **Petioles** 4 cm, slender

Immature ♂ catkins (above) 2 cm, hang at shoot tip. **Shoot** glabrous, zig-zagged

Seed (above) 2 mm, ripe by Sept, has 2 large wings **Bract** 7 mm, 3-lobed

'Dalecarlica': Shoots long, very pendulous

With a wide natural distribution throughout most of Europe and Asia Minor, Silver birch is recognizable by its distinctive bark and hairless twigs. It thrives on light, dry and sandy soils, dislikes shade and is plentiful on heaths and moorlands. 'Dalecarlica', from southern Sweden, is one of its graceful cultivars.

Paper birch

Betula papyrifera

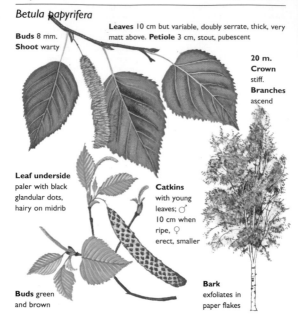

Buds 8 mm. **Shoot** warty

Leaves 10 cm but variable, doubly serrate, thick, very matt above. **Petiole** 3 cm, stout, pubescent

20 m. Crown stiff. **Branches** ascend

Leaf underside paler with black glandular dots, hairy on midrib

Catkins with young leaves; ♂ 10 cm when ripe, ♀ erect, smaller

Buds green and brown

Bark exfoliates in paper flakes

Paper birch grows throughout Canada and northern USA; its creamy or pinkish white bark was once used by Indians to cover their canoes. Szechuan birch (*B. szechuanica*) has a chalky white bark and leathery, 12 cm leaves, glaucous below.

Downy birch

Betula pubescens

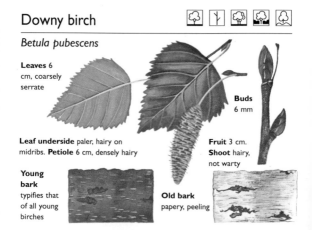

Leaves 6 cm, coarsely serrate

Buds 6 mm

Leaf underside paler, hairy on midribs. **Petiole** 6 cm, densely hairy

Young bark typifies that of all young birches

Fruit 3 cm. **Shoot** hairy, not warty

Old bark papery, peeling

Downy birch is identifiable by its hairy twigs and is more tolerant of climatic extremes than Silver birch. The 15 cm, doubly serrate leaves of Erman birch (*B. ermanii*), from Japan, are shiny below and have 7–11 pairs of veins.

Himalayan birch

Betula utilis

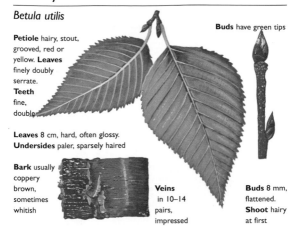

Buds have green tips

Petiole hairy, stout, grooved, red or yellow. **Leaves** finely doubly serrate.
Teeth fine, double

Leaves 8 cm, hard, often glossy.
Undersides paler, sparsely haired

Bark usually coppery brown, sometimes whitish

Veins in 10–14 pairs, impressed

Buds 8 mm, flattened.
Shoot hairy at first

Recognizable by its shoot, buds and vein count, Himalayan birch has a variably coloured bark which peels away in large sheets. That of Jacquemont birch (*B. jacquemontii*) is bright white while its coarsely serrate leaves have only 7–9 pairs of veins.

Yellow birch

Betula allegheniensis (syn. *B. lutea*)

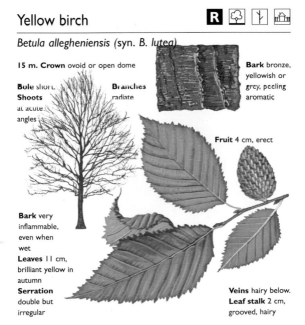

15 m. Crown ovoid or open dome

Bark bronze, yellowish or grey, peeling aromatic

Bole short.
Shoots at acute angles

Branches radiate

Fruit 4 cm, erect

Bark very inflammable, even when wet
Leaves 11 cm, brilliant yellow in autumn
Serration double but irregular

Veins hairy below.
Leaf stalk 2 cm, grooved, hairy

Native to eastern North America where it can reach 30 m, this birch is notable for its yellow autumn foliage and the long hairs of its leaves and young shoots. Cherry birch (*B. lenta*) has larger, more regularly toothed cordate leaves and thicker, black bark.

Alder

Alnus glutinosa

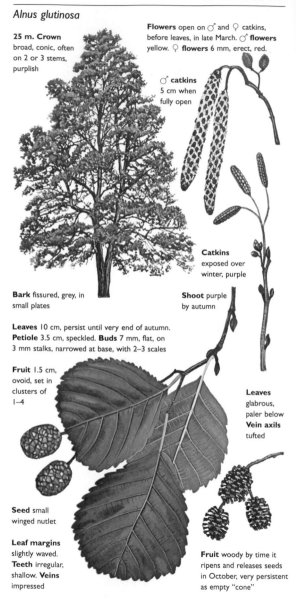

25 m. Crown broad, conic, often on 2 or 3 stems, purplish

Flowers open on ♂ and ♀ catkins, before leaves, in late March. ♂ **flowers** yellow. ♀ **flowers** 6 mm, erect, red.

♂ catkins 5 cm when fully open

Catkins exposed over winter, purple

Shoot purple by autumn

Bark fissured, grey, in small plates

Leaves 10 cm, persist until very end of autumn. **Petiole** 3.5 cm, speckled. **Buds** 7 mm, flat, on 3 mm stalks, narrowed at base, with 2–3 scales

Fruit 1.5 cm, ovoid, set in clusters of 1–4

Leaves glabrous, paler below **Vein axils** tufted

Seed small winged nutlet

Leaf margins slightly waved. **Teeth** irregular, shallow. **Veins** impressed

Fruit woody by time it ripens and releases seeds in October, very persistent as empty "cone"

Alders grow in damp locations and have buoyant seeds that are distributed by water. The deep roots help to conserve river banks and improve the soil with their nitrogen-fixing nodules. The tree survives happily on drier sites but does not regenerate there. 'Laciniata' and 'Imperalis' are forms with deeply lobed leaves.

Grey alder

Alnus incana

Petiole 3 cm

♂ **catkins**
10 cm

Leaves 10 cm, pointed, strongly toothed, sometimes lobulate. **Veins** in 7–12 pairs

♂ **catkins** in February

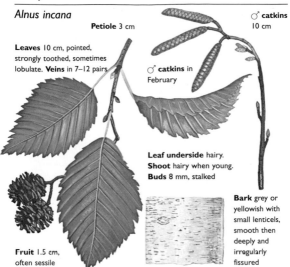

Leaf underside hairy.
Shoot hairy when young.
Buds 8 mm, stalked

Bark grey or yellowish with small lenticels, smooth then deeply and irregularly fissured

Fruit 1.5 cm, often sessile

Grey alder is widely planted on reclaimed sites and can be identified by its pubescent young shoots and the downy undersides of its leaves. Red alder (*A. rubra*) has larger and narrower, distinctly lobed leaves and angled, glabrous shoots.

Italian alder

Alnus cordata

Leaf 8 cm, cordate

♂ **catkin**
10 cm

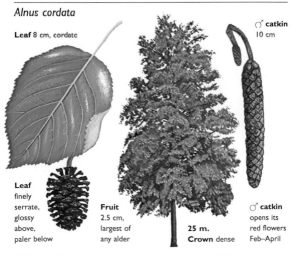

Leaf finely serrate, glossy above, paler below

Fruit 2.5 cm, largest of any alder

25 m.
Crown dense

♂ **catkin** opens its red flowers Feb–April

With a tolerance of urban atmospheres and an ability to grow on drier sites than other alders, this species makes an attractive street tree. It is notable for its almost pear-like leaves with orange axil tufts, sticky twigs and buds and large "cones".

Hazel

Corylus avellana

♂ **Catkins** 5 cm, open Feb. ♀ **catkins** 5 mm

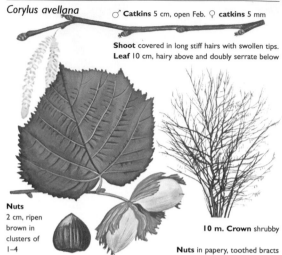

Shoot covered in long stiff hairs with swollen tips.
Leaf 10 cm, hairy above and doubly serrate below

Nuts
2 cm, ripen
brown in
clusters of
1–4

10 m. Crown shrubby

Nuts in papery, toothed bracts

Hazel is a small shrubby tree native to almost all Europe and recognized by its nuts, densely haired twigs and leaves and its plump male catkins. Its female catkins are small and have red styles. 'Contorta' with twisted stems, is a useful ornamental.

Turkish hazel

Corylus colurna

Leaf
15 cm,
cordate,
glossy

25 m. Crown regular
conic. **Branches** very
level, stout, twisting

Leaf sharply serrate.
Nuts 3 cm, almost covered
by thick, haired husk

Bole stout. **Shoots**
develop corky ridges.
Bark scaly

Turkish hazel is the most tree-like of the genus and its long, deeply lobed bracts (or cupules) almost cover the nuts. Filbert (*C. maxima*), also from the Balkans, has tubular, papery ones almost twice as long as the nuts.

Hornbeam

Carpinus betulus

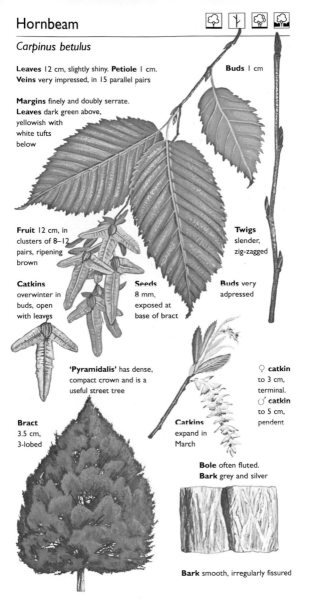

Leaves 12 cm, slightly shiny. **Petiole** 1 cm.
Veins very impressed, in 15 parallel pairs

Buds 1 cm

Margins finely and doubly serrate.
Leaves dark green above,
yellowish with
white tufts
below

Fruit 12 cm, in
clusters of 8–12
pairs, ripening
brown

Twigs
slender,
zig-zagged

Catkins
overwinter in
buds, open
with leaves

Seeds
8 mm,
exposed at
base of bract

Buds very
adpressed

'Pyramidalis' has dense,
compact crown and is a
useful street tree

♀ **catkin**
to 3 cm,
terminal.
♂ **catkin**
to 5 cm,
pendent

Bract
3.5 cm,
3-lobed

Catkins
expand in
March

Bole often fluted.
Bark grey and silver

Bark smooth, irregularly fissured

Hornbeam is sometimes mistaken for Beech (p 94) but closer
scrutiny reveals its leaves to be serrate and have parallel and
deeply impressed veins. Its smaller buds are set very closely
against the shoots; its fruit is very different from that of Beech.
Hornbeam is a forest and hedgerow tree that was once rigorously
pollarded and coppiced for firewood and highly valued for the
hardness and smoothness of its timber.

Beech and oak family *Fagaceae*

The members of this large, mainly temperate family have simple and alternate leaves and fruit in the form of nuts. These are either fully enclosed by an involucre (or cupule) of fused bracts as in *Fagus*, *Nothofagus* (pp 96–7) and *Castanea* (p 105), or merely supported by it as in *Quercus* (pp 98–104). Male and female flowers are carried in separate catkins on the same tree.

Beech

Fagus sylvatica

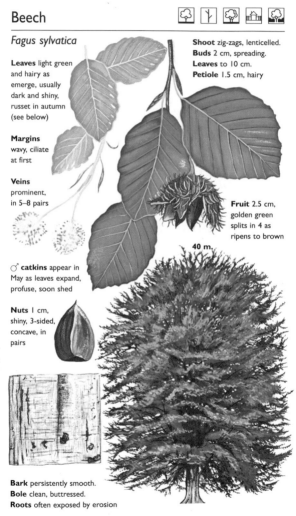

Leaves light green and hairy as emerge, usually dark and shiny, russet in autumn (see below)

Margins wavy, ciliate at first

Veins prominent, in 5–8 pairs

♂ **catkins** appear in May as leaves expand, profuse, soon shed

Nuts I cm, shiny, 3-sided, concave, in pairs

Shoot zig-zags, lenticelled.
Buds 2 cm, spreading.
Leaves to 10 cm.
Petiole I.5 cm, hairy

Fruit 2.5 cm, golden green splits in 4 as ripens to brown

40 m.

Bark persistently smooth.
Bole clean, buttressed.
Roots often exposed by erosion

This majestic tree is instantly recognizable by its smooth bark. Although its natural range includes most of continental Europe and southern Britain, it has been widely planted elsewhere for its timber, and thrives on chalk and limestone. Oriental beech (*F. orientalis*), from the Balkans and Asia Minor, has leafy cupules and broader, larger leaves which have 7–10 pairs of veins.

Some cultivars of Beech

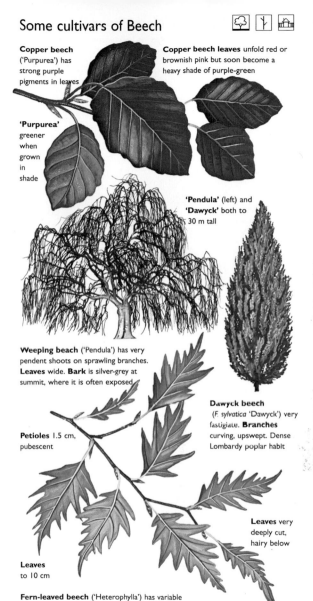

Copper beech ('Purpurea') has strong purple pigments in leaves

Copper beech leaves unfold red or brownish pink but soon become a heavy shade of purple-green

'Purpurea' greener when grown in shade

'Pendula' (left) and **'Dawyck'** both to 30 m tall

Weeping beach ('Pendula') has very pendent shoots on sprawling branches. **Leaves** wide. **Bark** is silver-grey at summit, where it is often exposed

Dawyck beech (*F. sylvatica* 'Dawyck') very fastigiate. **Branches** curving, upswept. Dense Lombardy poplar habit

Petioles 1.5 cm, pubescent

Leaves very deeply cut, hairy below

Leaves to 10 cm

Fern-leaved beech ('Heterophylla') has variable leaves, sometimes willow-like

Beech is noted for the variety of its cultivars. Copper beech, the most common, may have deep purple ('Purpurea') or red leaved clones. Weeping and Dawyck beeches have distinctive habits, 'Heterophylla' remarkable leaves. Others include 'Zlatia', with new foliage golden until July, and 'Rotundifolia' with small, almost round leaves and variegated forms.

Southern beeches *Nothofagus*

Nothofagus contains about 40 species, all native to the southern hemisphere and usually differing from true beeches in their smaller fruits with 3 to 7 nutlets, rounder buds, and much smaller, evergreen leaves. Most species are evergreen.

Rauli

Nothofagus nervosa (syn. *N. procera*)

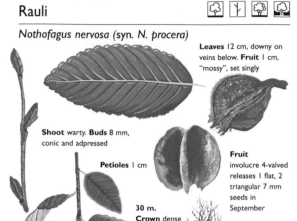

Leaves 12 cm, downy on veins below. **Fruit** 1 cm, "mossy", set singly

Shoot warty. **Buds** 8 mm, conic and adpressed

Petioles 1 cm

Fruit involucre 4-valved releases 1 flat, 2 triangular 7 mm seeds in September

30 m. Crown dense

Branches stout, ascend steeply, whorled when young. **Bark** dull, fissured

Veins impressed, in 15–18 pairs

Margins slightly waved, very finely toothed

Leaves have rounded bases and acute or rounded tips. **Venation** very prominent. **New leaves** coppery. **Autumn leaves** golden red

Rauli, from the Chilean Andes, is being increasingly planted in the northern hemisphere both for its vigour – on good, well-drained, frost-free sites it can grow 2 m a year – and for the excellent potential of its timber. It can be distinguished from Roblé beech by its stouter shoots, larger and more pointed buds and the more numerous veins of its leaves.

Roblé beech

Nothofagus obliqua

Margins are irregularly toothed. **Veins** extend to tips of teeth

Veins in 7–11 pairs. **Shoot** slender

Petiole 5 mm, red

Fruit 8 cm, set singly, ribbed, has 3 seeds

Buds 5 mm, spreading

30 m. Crown ovoid, spreading. **Bark** fissured

The Chilean Roblé beech is as vigorous as Rauli but will tolerate drier sites. Antarctic beech (*N. antarctica*) forms a smaller tree, to 15 m, and has crinkled, almost sessile, glossy leaves. These have four pairs of veins which end between two teeth.

Coigue

Nothofagus dombeyi

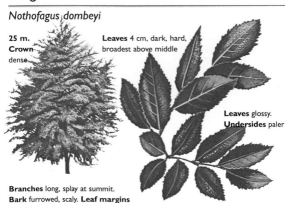

25 m. Crown dense

Leaves 4 cm, dark, hard, broadest above middle

Leaves glossy. **Undersides** paler

Branches long, splay at summit. **Bark** furrowed, scaly. **Leaf margins** finely, unevenly serrate

Buds 1 mm

Coigue is a hardy evergreen from Chile and Argentina. Red beech (*N. fusca*) from New Zealand is also evergreen and has thin, ovate leaves 5 cm long, with coarser, rounded teeth and three or four pairs of veins. They turn red before falling.

Oaks *Quercus*

This large and important group of noble trees comprises over 400 separate species as well as many hybrids and is found throughout the temperate areas of Europe, Asia and North America. All oaks are noted for their acorns which may ripen over either one or two years and provide the best means of identification. Another is the arrangement of leaves and buds which cluster at the end of shoots and separate *Quercus* from most other genera. Oaks have separate male and female flowers appearing on the same tree; the females are erect but inconspicuous while the males appear in long, pendulous catkins at the same time as the new leaves open. The genus contains both deciduous and evergreen species.

Sessile oak

Quercus petraea (syn. *Q. sessiliflora*)

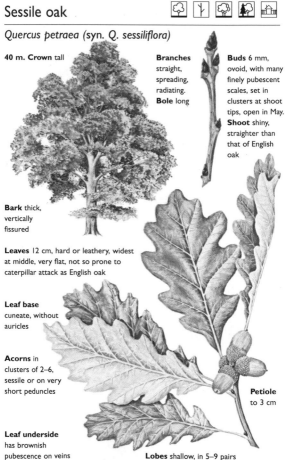

40 m. Crown tall

Branches straight, spreading, radiating.
Bole long

Buds 6 mm, ovoid, with many finely pubescent scales, set in clusters at shoot tips, open in May.
Shoot shiny, straighter than that of English oak

Bark thick, vertically fissured

Leaves 12 cm, hard or leathery, widest at middle, very flat, not so prone to caterpillar attack as English oak

Leaf base cuneate, without auricles

Acorns in clusters of 2–6, sessile or on very short peduncles

Petiole to 3 cm

Leaf underside has brownish pubescence on veins

Lobes shallow, in 5–9 pairs

With a long bole that extends well into the crown, this oak can be further distinguished from English oak by its almost stalkless, slightly smaller acorns and the wedge-shaped bases of its leaves. It grows well on light, acidic, stony soil. The similar Downy oak (*Q. pubescens*) has densely hairy leaves and shoots.

English oak

Quercus robur (Syn. Q. pedunculata)

35 m. Crown wide

Foliage set in bunches

Branches large and heavy, very irregular, bear sprouts

Crown irregularly domed.
Bole short, very stout.
Bark fissures Into tiers of rectangular plates

Leaves have auricles at bases.
Leaf stalk I cm

Lobes in 4 or 5 pairs, deeply cut

Leaves to 12 cm, widest above middle

Acorns 2.5 cm, usually in pairs on long, thin peduncle to 10 cm

Cypress oak
(Q. robur 'Fastigiata') has upswept crown, narrow when young; grows in central Europe

English oak is very common throughout Europe. It thrives on heavy clay but will do equally well elsewhere including the lighter, stonier soil favoured by *Q. petraea*. Unlike Sessile oak its leaves are glabrous below and have auricles at their bases. Its acorns are carried on long stalks and give the tree its alternative name of Pedunculate oak. Many predators such as the larvae of the Purple hairstreak butterfly (*Quercusia quercus*) attack its young foliage but do no permanent damage since further flushes of growth occur until September.

Turkey oak

Quercus cerris

Stipules long, 2.5 cm, around *all* buds.
Shoot pubescent

Bark fissures shallow; deeper and plating on old trees

Acorn large, 2.5 cm, in sessile, "mossy" cup whose 4 mm filaments are parted, pointing upwards on upper half of cup

Leaves 13 cm, very variable, rough, glossy above, grey, downy below. **Lobes** angular, usually in 5–9 pairs

This hardy native of southern and south-west Europe naturalizes easily and grows vigorously into a mature and massively domed tree which can reach 40 m. It is more upright than *Q. robur* (p 99); unlike all other oaks, it has stipules arranged round *all* its buds.

Lucombe oak

Quercus x *hispanica* 'Lucombeana'

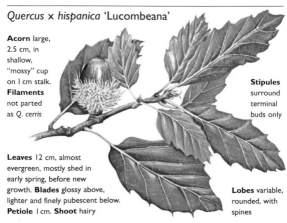

Acorn large, 2.5 cm, in shallow, "mossy" cup on 1 cm stalk.
Filaments not parted as *Q. cerris*

Stipules surround terminal buds only

Leaves 12 cm, almost evergreen, mostly shed in early spring, before new growth. **Blades** glossy above, lighter and finely pubescent below. **Petiole** 1 cm. **Shoot** hairy

Lobes variable, rounded, with spines

Lucombe oak is a form of the natural but variable hybrid of Turkey oak and Cork oak (p 102), inheriting the habit, leaf shape, stipulate buds and acorns of the former species and the bark and semi-green nature of the latter. This tree was first raised by William Lucombe, an Exeter nurseryman, in about 1765.

Algerian oak

Quercus canariensis

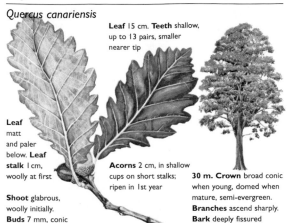

Leaf 15 cm. **Teeth** shallow, up to 13 pairs, smaller nearer tip

Leaf matt and paler below. **Leaf stalk** 1 cm, woolly at first

Acorns 2 cm, in shallow cups on short stalks; ripen in 1st year

Shoot glabrous, woolly initially. **Buds** 7 mm, conic

30 m. Crown broad conic when young, domed when mature, semi-evergreen. **Branches** ascend sharply. **Bark** deeply fissured

One of the largest trees to retain a proportion of green leaves throughout the winter, this species is native to north Africa, Spain and Portugal. Caucasian oak (*Q. macranthera*) is similar but its wholly deciduous leaves have more rounded lobes and it carries dark red, shiny buds on pubescent shoots.

Hungarian oak

Quercus frainetto

Buds large, to 1 cm, with many downy scales. **Shoot** downy becoming glabrous; ridged when tree young

Lobes large, in 7–11 pairs, with lobulate margins. **Sinuses** the most deeply cut of any European oak

Leaves large, to 25 cm, with basal auricles. **Blade** sub-glossy above, hairy below. **Petiole** 1 cm, pubescent

30 m. Crown strongly domed. **Branches** radiate. **Bole** stout. **Bark** dark, fissured

Native to south-eastern Europe, this vigorous species is unmistakable in its boldly lobed foliage. Its acorns, similar to those of Algerian oak, ripen in one year. The American White oak (*Q. alba*) also has large, deeply cut leaves but their lobes are more rounded and their petioles up to 2.5 cm long.

Cork oak

Quercus suber

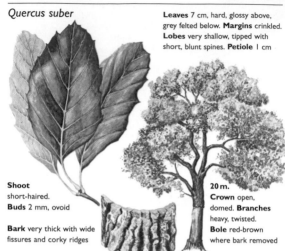

Leaves 7 cm, hard, glossy above, grey felted below. **Margins** crinkled. **Lobes** very shallow, tipped with short, blunt spines. **Petiole** 1 cm

Shoot short-haired. **Buds** 2 mm, ovoid

Bark very thick with wide fissures and corky ridges

20 m. Crown open, domed. **Branches** heavy, twisted. **Bole** red-brown where bark removed

The leaves of this Mediterranean tree resemble those of Holm and Turkey oaks (p 100). Its useful bark, harvested commercially about every ten years, is similar to that of Lucombe oak (p 100) and Chinese cork oak (*Q. variabilis*) whose wholly deciduous leaves have filamented teeth and are silvery-grey below.

Holm oak

Quercus ilex

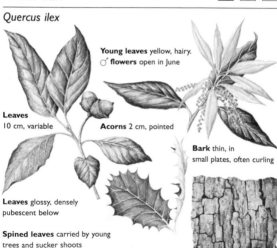

Young leaves yellow, hairy. ♂ **flowers** open in June

Leaves 10 cm, variable

Acorns 2 cm, pointed

Bark thin, in small plates, often curling

Leaves glossy, densely pubescent below

Spined leaves carried by young trees and sucker shoots

A broadly domed species reaching up to 30 m, the sombre Holm oak becomes brighter for a brief period in June when its new, yellowish leaves open. Kermes oak (*Q. coccifera*) is another native of the Mediterranean and hosts the Kermes insect from which scarlet grain dye is prepared. Its leaves are Holly-like.

Red oak

Quercus rubra

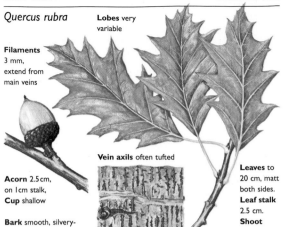

Lobes very variable

Filaments 3 mm, extend from main veins

Vein axils often tufted

Acorn 2.5 cm, on 1 cm stalk, **Cup** shallow

Bark smooth, silvery-grey, becoming fissured

Leaves to 20 cm, matt both sides. **Leaf stalk** 2.5 cm. **Shoot** ridged

Glorious in the autumnal hues which give it its name, this sturdy species from the eastern USA typifies a large group of New World oaks which have filamented leaves and smoothish barks. Red oak has heavy branches and grows vigorously to produce a broadly domed crown reaching 35 m.

Scarlet oak

Quercus coccinea

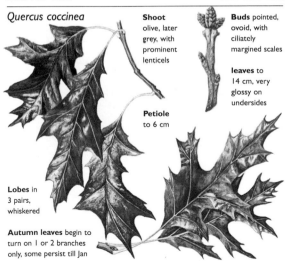

Shoot olive, later grey, with prominent lenticels

Buds pointed, ovoid, with ciliately margined scales

leaves to 14 cm, very glossy on undersides

Petiole to 6 cm

Lobes in 3 pairs, whiskered

Autumn leaves begin to turn on 1 or 2 branches only, some persist till Jan

A native of eastern North America, Scarlet oak usually has less intense autumnal foliage when grown in Europe, and is less common than Red oak from which it can be distinguished by its smaller, glossy, more deeply lobed leaves and smaller acorns. Its bud scales have pubescent margins and it grows to 25 m.

Pin oak

Quercus palustris

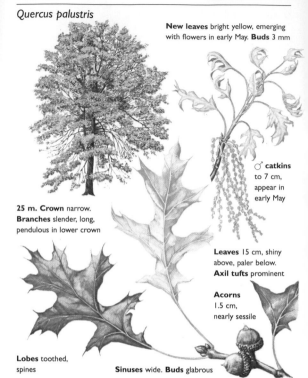

New leaves bright yellow, emerging with flowers in early May. **Buds** 3 mm

♂ **catkins** to 7 cm, appear in early May

25 m. Crown narrow. **Branches** slender, long, pendulous in lower crown

Leaves 15 cm, shiny above, paler below. **Axil tufts** prominent

Acorns 1.5 cm, nearly sessile

Lobes toothed, spines

Sinuses wide. **Buds** glabrous

Small pin-like branches which sometimes grow on its bole help to identify this tree in winter. Its prominent axillary tufts and its shallow acorn cups are also distinctive. Pin oak's narrowly lobed leaves turn red in autumn but not as richly as some of its cousins. Northern pin oak (*Q. ellipsoidalis*) has sessile acorns to 2.5 cm.

Willow oak

Quercus phellos

Acorn 1 cm, nearly sessile

Leaf 12 cm. **Petiole** 4 mm

Leaves entire

From the south-eastern USA. Willow oak has foliage which opens yellow and becomes golden in autumn. Schoch oak (*Q. x schochiana*) is its hybrid with Pin oak and has leaves with one or two lobes. Shingle oak (*Q. imbricaria*) has wider, entire leaves.

Sweet chestnut

Castanea sativa

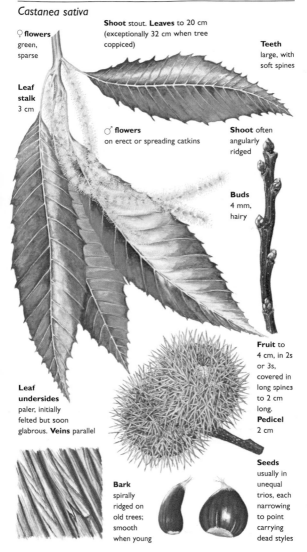

♀ **flowers** green, sparse

Leaf stalk 3 cm

Shoot stout. **Leaves** to 20 cm (exceptionally 32 cm when tree coppiced)

Teeth large, with soft spines

♂ **flowers** on erect or spreading catkins

Shoot often angularly ridged

Buds 4 mm, hairy

Leaf undersides paler, initially felted but soon glabrous. **Veins** parallel

Fruit to 4 cm, in 2s or 3s, covered in long spines to 2 cm long. **Pedicel** 2 cm

Bark spirally ridged on old trees; smooth when young

Seeds usually in unequal trios, each narrowing to point carrying dead styles

This Mediterranean tree has a crown which can reach 30 m and a girth that can sometimes exceed 13 m. Exceptional in its vigour, it is often grown for the strong shoots it produces when coppiced. Although closely related to the oaks it differs from them in the female flowers it carries at the base of some male catkins. They open in late June, well after the leaves have appeared. Its buds are not carried in terminal clusters like those of *Quercus*, two members of which, Lebanon oak (*Q. lihani*) and Chestnut-leaved oak (*Q. castaneifolia*) have similar leaves to Sweet chestnut.

Laurel family *Lauraceae*

This is a large mainly warm temperate and tropical family of trees and shrubs with aromatic foliage. The fruit is a single seeded drupe or berry.

Bay laurel, Poets laurel, Sweet bay

Laurus nobilis

Fruit ovoid berry, shiny green until ripening black, 1.0–1.5 cm

Petiole 0.5–1 cm

Habit conical to broad conic, often on several stems, to 20 m

Leaves elliptic, pointed, strongly aromatic especially when crushed or handled, dark glossy green above with pale veins and a pale untoothed crinkled margin, underside light green, 5–13 cm by 2–5 cm

Flowers in leaf axilis in June

Shoot green
Buds conic, 0.3 cm

Bay laurel is native to the Mediterranean region, where it occurs in evergreen forests. The foliage was used to make the wreaths given to conquering generals and favoured poets by ancient Greeks and Romans. This practice lives on in the degree of bachelor, derived from "baccalaureus" or laurel berries via the French bachelier.

California laurel

Umbellularia californica

Leaves 15 cm, oblong-lanceolate or elliptic, dark, lustrous above, dull paler below.

25 m. Crown a dense, rounded dome, often on several stems

Bark dark red-brown, thin, smooth

Leaves flat, glabrous, evergreen, turning yellow when shed in second year.
Margins entire, down-turned.
Midrib whitish.
Apex either acute or rounded.
Leaf base cuneate. **Petiole** 6 mm, slender

Bud naked

Fruit to 5 cm, in umbels of 2–3, a subglobose berry, green ripening to purple. **Flesh** thin. **Seed** brown, smooth

Shoot hairy at first, yellow, later brown, glabrous

This is the only species in this genus, named after its pale yellow flowers which appear in early spring in small umbels; it is also known as "Headache tree" because of the unpleasant effect of too much sniffing of its aromatic foliage.

Sassafras

Sassafras albidum

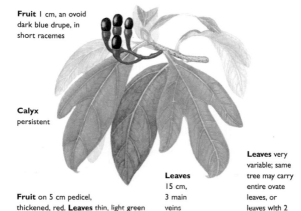

Shoot shiny, brittle, rather glaucous bright green, marked with elevated leaf scars. **Bud** I cm

Fruit I cm, an ovoid dark blue drupe, in short racemes

Calyx persistent

Leaves very variable; same tree may carry entire ovate leaves, or leaves with 2 or 3 lobes

Leaves 15 cm, 3 main veins

Fruit on 5 cm pedicel, thickened, red. **Leaves** thin, light green above, glaucous below. **Petiole** 3 cm

This freely suckering tree grows to 25 m with an open, flat-topped crown and closely furrowed dark brown bark. It is a native of the eastern USA, and the aromatic twigs, bark and roots have long been used to produce a fragrant oil or tea.

Spur leaf

Tetracentron sinense

Leaves ovate, with a long slender tip, base cordate, margin with small teeth, veins impressed above, raised beneath

Buds long conic or spike shaped, alternate, 1.0–1.5 cm

Flowers and fruits in pendent slender catkins 8–15 cm

Petiole grooved, green or pink, enclosing the buds, 2.5–5 cm

Shoot green or pink

Spur leaf is distributed from central China south to Vietnam and west along the Himalayas to Mepal. It has leaves which are similar to *Cercidiphyllum* (p 115) but instantly recognisable in their being alternate on the shoot. The fruits have many small four horned capsules with minute seeds.

Elm family *Ulmaceae*

This distinctive group of trees and shrubs is found in both hemispheres and comprises about 15 genera of which *Ulmus* and *Zelkova* are the two most frequently encountered in Europe. The family is characterized by undivided, usually oblique, leaves that are carried alternately and often have rough surfaces and buds with overlapping scales. Its flowers are usually perfect, have many stamens and appear with or before the leaves. Their ovaries have one ovule. Elms have fruit in the form of a broad samara; that of zelkovas is a small nutlet. The other genus which may be encountered is *Celtis*, whose leaves are strongly three-veined from the base and a fruit which is a small round green drupe on a 1 cm pedicel.

Dutch elm disease

This disease is caused by a fungus but spread by elm bark beetles, with secondary infections caused through root grafts. The beetles breed in dying or recently dead mature bark, producing characteristic galleries between the wood and the bark. The emerging beetles carry the fungal spores off to living trees where they feed on twigs.

English elm

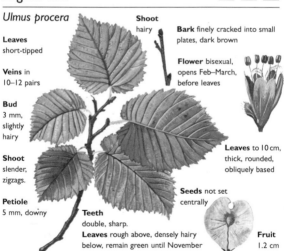

Ulmus procera

Leaves short-tipped

Veins in 10–12 pairs

Bud 3 mm, slightly hairy

Shoot slender, zigzags.

Petiole 5 mm, downy

Shoot hairy

Bark finely cracked into small plates, dark brown

Flower bisexual, opens Feb–March, before leaves

Leaves to 10 cm, thick, rounded, obliquely based

Seeds not set centrally

Teeth double, sharp.

Leaves rough above, densely hairy below, remain green until November

Fruit 1.2 cm

From the 18th century until the 1970's this was a common hedgerow tree over much of England, with majestic trees such as the one illustrated in the frontispiece on page 1. Since then, the tree has been restricted by Dutch elm disease to small trees with ovoid crowns to 12 m. Its origins, however, are an enigma; it was either a very early introduction or may have arisen as a hybrid. Fertile seeds are rarely (if ever) set and reproduction is entirely by root suckers. Fluttering elm (*U. laens*) from continental Europe has very long peduncles.

Wych elm

Ulmus glabra

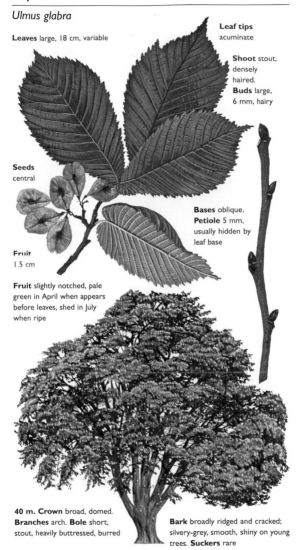

Leaves large, 18 cm, variable

Leaf tips acuminate

Shoot stout, densely haired.
Buds large, 6 mm, hairy

Seeds central

Bases oblique.
Petiole 5 mm, usually hidden by leaf base

Fruit 1.5 cm

Fruit slightly notched, pale green in April when appears before leaves, shed in July when ripe

40 m. Crown broad, domed.
Branches arch. **Bole** short, stout, heavily buttressed, burred

Bark broadly ridged and cracked; silvery-grey, smooth, shiny on young trees. **Suckers** rare

Although sometimes shrubby on exposed sites, Wych elm is renowned for its majestic, spreading crown which is especially attractive in autumn. Its botanical name derives from the smoothness of its *young* bark and not from the leaves, which are very rough above. Most Wych elm seeds are fertile and it very rarely produces suckers. The fruit, appearing well before the foliage, is often produced so abundantly that the tree appears to be fully clothed. It is native to most of Europe and western Asia and the only elm unquestionably indigenous to Britain.

Smooth-leaved elm

Ulmus carpinifolia (syn. U. minor)

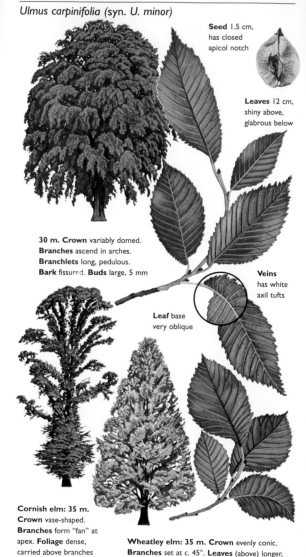

Seed 1.5 cm, has closed apicol notch

Leaves 12 cm, shiny above, glabrous below

30 m. Crown variably domed. **Branches** ascend in arches. **Branchlets** long, pedulous. **Bark** fissured. **Buds** large, 5 mm

Veins has white axil tufts

Leaf base very oblique

Cornish elm: 35 m. Crown vase-shaped. **Branches** form "fan" at apex. **Foliage** dense, carried above branches

Wheatley elm: 35 m. Crown evenly conic. **Branches** set at c. 45°. **Leaves** (above) longer, rounder than Cornish elm

Native to most of Europe, this hedgerow tree was probably introduced to southern Britain as a boundary marker in the first century BC and regional varieties – sometimes classified as species – have developed since then. Those most often seen are Wheatley (or Jersey) elm (*U.c.* var. *sarniensis*) which occurs "wild" in south-west England and southern Ireland. Its leaves are cupped and smaller than those of Wheatley elm.

Huntingdon elm

Ulmus x hollandica 'Vegeta'

U. x *hollandica* covers all the natural hybrids between *U. glabra* (p 109) and *U. carpinifolia*. First propagated in 1760, this magnificent tree can be identified by the very oblique bases of its large, doubly serrate leaves and the brown axil tufts of their undersides. It is one of the forms more resistant to Dutch elm disease.

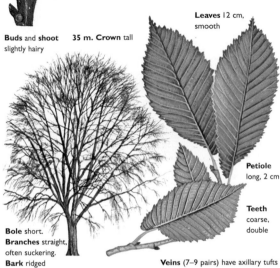

Leaves 12 cm, smooth

Buds and **shoot** slightly hairy

35 m. Crown tall

Petiole long, 2 cm

Teeth coarse, double

Bole short.
Branches straight, often suckering.
Bark ridged

Veins (7–9 pairs) have axillary tufts

Siberian elm

Ulmus pumila

Teeth small, irregular, rounded

Blades taper to acute apexes

Bases round or slightly oblique

Buds very small, 2 mm

Veins impressed, in 10–12 pairs. **Petiole** long, 5 mm

Leaves to 7 cm

Almost evergreen and apparently very resistant to Dutch elm disease, Siberian elm grows fairly quickly into a small, flat-domed, leafy tree. Chinese elm (*U. parvifolia*) has much smaller, greener leaves, hairy shoots and flowers in September.

Caucasian elm

Zelkova carpinifolia

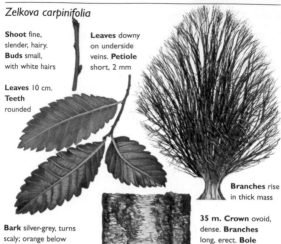

Shoot fine, slender, hairy. **Buds** small, with white hairs

Leaves downy on underside veins. **Petiole** short, 2 mm

Leaves 10 cm. **Teeth** rounded

Branches rise in thick mass

Bark silver-grey, turns scaly; orange below exfoliating scales

35 m. Crown ovoid, dense. **Branches** long, erect. **Bole** short, stout, fluted

Perhaps the most common member of the hardy *Zelkova* genus, Caucasian elm has smaller leaves with more rounded teeth than Keaki, with which it is sometimes confused, and a distinctive habit. Cretan zelkova (*Z. abelicea*) is a small tree or shrub whose 3 cm leaves are nearly sessile. Its fruit is downy.

Keaki

Zelkova serrata

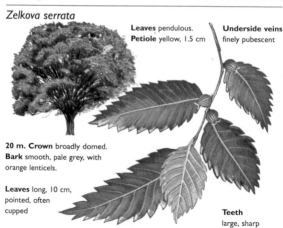

Leaves pendulous. **Petiole** yellow, 1.5 cm

Underside veins finely pubescent

20 m. Crown broadly domed. **Bark** smooth, pale grey, with orange lenticels.

Leaves long, 10 cm, pointed, often cupped

Teeth large, sharp

Much prized in its native Japan for the quality of its timber, Keaki shares the steel-grey and orange bark of Caucasian elm but is a less imposing tree. Its larger leaves have pointed teeth and longer petioles and assume autumn shades of yellow, pink and bronze. Its fine zig-zagged shoots carry minute 1 mm buds.

Mulberry family *Moraceae*

All the members of this family have milky saps but differ in the way their fleshy fruit develops. In *Morus*, this is a cluster of drupes evolving from its flower sepals whereas the flesh of *Broussonetia's* fruit derives from the stalk of the ovary.

Mulberry

Morus nigra

Buds 6 mm, shiny, red or purplish-brown

Shoot stout, hairy, with large lenticels

10 m. Crown low, rounded. **Branches** twisted. **Bole** short, often leans. **Bark** stringy, fissured, orange-brown, with many burrs

Fruit 1.5 cm, ripens from green to red, then finally purplish-black by late August

Leaves 15 cm, rough, glossy and hairy above, paler, downy below. **Petiole** 2 cm, stout, hairy

Leaf deeply cordate, occasionally 3-lobed

Leaves often curled

Believed to be of Chinese origin, Black mulberry has been cultivated for thousands of years for its sweet but tangy raspberry-like fruit. It has been widely planted in Europe and is usually propagated from cuttings. From Japan and China, Paper mulberry (*Broussonetia papyrifera*) has leaves which resemble those of Mulberry but are densely downy below; its fruit and catkins hang in globular heads. The bark is made into cloth and paper.

White mulberry

Morus alba

Leaves 3-lobed on strong shoots. **Bases** cordate. **Apexes** acute or rounded. **Margins** coarsely toothed

Shoots initially hairy, soon glabrous, slender. **Buds** smaller than Black mulberry, conical

Leaves 20 cm, shiny green, smooth, finely haired below. **Petiole** 2.5 cm

Fruit 2.5 cm, sweet

White mulberry is a small Chinese tree reaching up to 16 m. It is the preferred food of the silkworm caterpillar for which it is cultivated in southern Europe. China and Japan. The fruit, although sweet, is insipid and not as agreeable as that of Black mulberry. It ripens from green to white, pinkish or violet purple.

Fig

Ficus carica

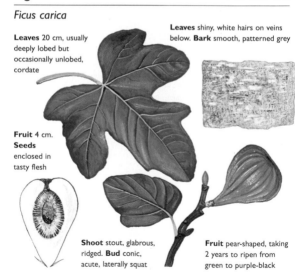

Leaves 20 cm, usually deeply lobed but occasionally unlobed, cordate

Leaves shiny, white hairs on veins below. **Bark** smooth, patterned grey

Fruit 4 cm. **Seeds** enclosed in tasty flesh

Shoot stout, glabrous, ridged. **Bud** conic, acute, laterally squat

Fruit pear-shaped, taking 2 years to ripen from green to purple-black

Southern European, this forms an 8 m spreading tree. It produces fruit from modified shoot tips, fertilization effected by a small wasp which breeds in the young fruit. In Britain, the wasp does not survive; only the Adriatic form, which needs no fertilizing, produces ripe fruit.

Katsura family *Cercidiphyllaceae*

Katsura

Cercidiphyllum japonicum

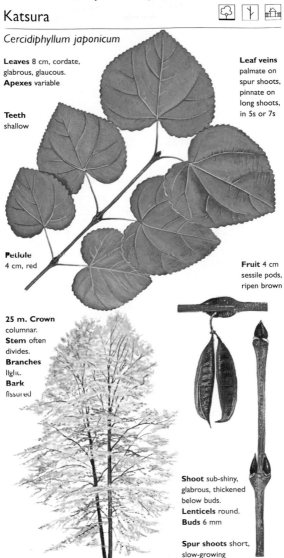

Leaves 8 cm, cordate, glabrous, glaucous.
Apexes variable

Teeth shallow

Leaf veins palmate on spur shoots, pinnate on long shoots, in 5s or 7s

Petiole 4 cm, red

Fruit 4 cm sessile pods, ripen brown

25 m. Crown columnar.
Stem often divides.
Branches light.
Bark fissured

Shoot sub-shiny, glabrous, thickened below buds.
Lenticels round.
Buds 6 mm

Spur shoots short, slow-growing

Katsura, native to central China and Japan, is noted for the brilliance of its autumn colour and for its bright pink young leaves which soon turn fresh green. Its leaves are similar to those of *Cercis* (p 145), hence *Cercidiphyllum* (= Ceris leaf), but it is actually in a different family which contains only one other species. This is *C. magnificum* which has larger leaves, two-winged seeds and is found only in Japan.

Magnolia family *Magnoliaceae*

Magnolia

Magnolia × soulangeana

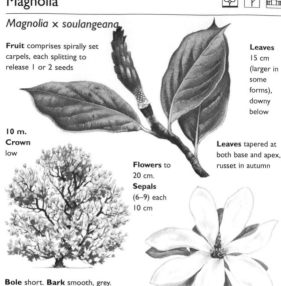

Fruit comprises spirally set carpels, each splitting to release 1 or 2 seeds

Leaves 15 cm (larger in some forms), downy below

Leaves tapered at both base and apex, russet in autumn

10 m. Crown low

Flowers to 20 cm. **Sepals** (6–9) each 10 cm

Bole short. **Bark** smooth, grey. **Flowers** before or with new leaves

The classic magnolia, first raised in France, is a hybrid of two wild Chinese species, *M. denudata* and *M. lilliflora*. The latter's 'Nigra' cultivar is compact and shrubby and often produces a second crop of its red-purple flowers in late summer.

Campbell magnolia

Magnolia campbellii

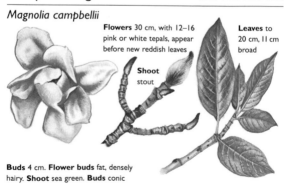

Flowers 30 cm, with 12–16 pink or white tepals, appear before new reddish leaves

Leaves to 20 cm, 11 cm broad

Shoot stout

Buds 4 cm. **Flower buds** fat, densely hairy. **Shoot** sea green. **Buds** conic

Between February and April, this Himalayan tree carries its magnificent flowers on bare shoots, as do two Chinese cousins, Sprenger magnolia (*M. sprengeri*), with broader leaves, and Sargent magnolia (*M. sargentiana*), with obliquely cuneate ones.

Southern magnolia

Magnolia grandiflora

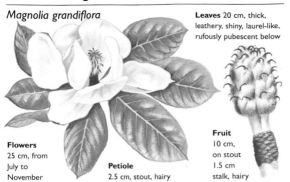

Leaves 20 cm, thick, leathery, shiny, laurel-like, rufously pubescent below

Flowers 25 cm, from July to November

Petiole 2.5 cm, stout, hairy

Fruit 10 cm, on stout 1.5 cm stalk, hairy

This small evergreen from the southern USA can be grown in less warm climates but may require the shelter of a wall to survive and flower. The Chinese Delavay magnolia (*M. delavayi*), also evergreen, has larger, very wide, matt, sea-green leaves.

Japanese magnolia

Magnolia kobus

Base branches regularly clothed in white flowers on older trees; younger trees shy to flower

Leaves 15 cm.
Shoot shiny, greenish-brown

Leaves crinkled, shiny below.
Veins impressed.
Petiole 1.5 cm

15 m. Crown of young trees broad and conic, becoming domed.
Branches level

Flowers 12 cm

Flowers carried profusely, appear in April, before leaves

This small species reaches 12 m and has slender, curved leaf buds and grey, downy flower buds. Its shoots are fragrant when crushed. *M. kobus* var. *borealis* is hardier and has pointed leaves. Those of Willow magnolia (*M. salicifolia*), also from Japan, are slender while its crown is an elegant, narrow dome.

Cucumber tree

Magnolia acuminata

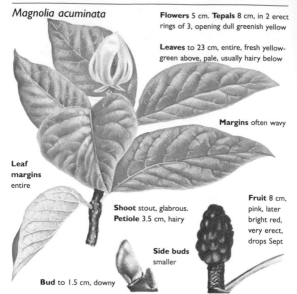

Flowers 5 cm. **Tepals** 8 cm, in 2 erect rings of 3, opening dull greenish yellow

Leaves to 23 cm, entire, fresh yellow-green above, pale, usually hairy below

Margins often wavy

Leaf margins entire

Shoot stout, glabrous. **Petiole** 3.5 cm, hairy

Side buds smaller

Fruit 8 cm, pink, later bright red, very erect, drops Sept

Bud to 1.5 cm, downy

From south-western USA and named after the resemblance of its young seed clusters to cucumbers, this stately tree grows to about 25 m. Wilson magnolia (*M. wilsonii*), from China, hardly reaches a third of this and produces hanging, pure white flowers.

Sweet bay

Magnolia virginiana

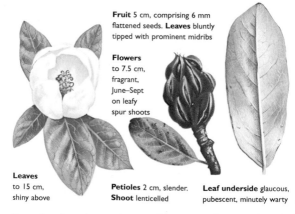

Fruit 5 cm, comprising 6 mm flattened seeds. **Leaves** bluntly tipped with prominent midribs

Flowers to 7.5 cm, fragrant, June–Sept on leafy spur shoots

Leaves to 15 cm, shiny above

Petioles 2 cm, slender. **Shoot** lenticelled

Leaf underside glaucous, pubescent, minutely warty

Sweet bay is native to the coastal swamps and rivers of south-eastern USA and evergreen in the southern part of this range. In the late seventeenth century it was the first magnolia grown in Europe where its small flowers sometimes persist till December.

Tulip tree

Liriodendron tulipifera

Buds 1 cm, flat, obovoid with 2 purple scales, stalked. **Shoot** shiny. **Leaf scars** very prominent

Leaves 15 cm, usually 4-lobed, glabrous, shiny, glaucous below

Petiole 10 cm, has 2 prominent stipules

35 m. Crown dense, becomes broader, more open with age. **Branches** regular

Native to eastern USA, this species has distinctive leaves and produces yellow-green tulip-shaped flowers in June, followed by erect, spindle-shaped fruits. Chinese tulip tree (*L. chinese*) has thinner leaves which are deeply lobed and minutely warted below.

Embrothrium family *Proteaceae*

Chilean firebush

Embrothrium coccineum

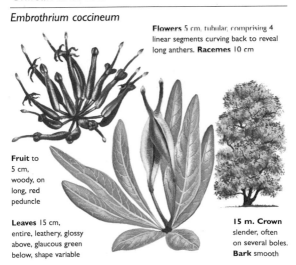

Flowers 5 cm, tubular, comprising 4 linear segments curving back to reveal long anthers. **Racemes** 10 cm

Fruit to 5 cm, woody, on long, red peduncle

Leaves 15 cm, entire, leathery, glossy above, glaucous green below, shape variable

15 m. Crown slender, often on several boles. **Bark** smooth

Chilean firebush is native to Chile and Argentina but grows in Europe as far north as Britain. It is a flamboyant sight in early summer when its newly-opened flowers contrast with the dark, glossy foliage; though vigorous, it is short-lived.

Witch-hazel family *Hamamelidaceae*

Sweet gum

Liquidambar styraciflua

30 m. Crown broad dome, ovoid-conic when young, turns orange, red or purple in autumn

Leaves 5 – rarely 7-lobed, 15 cm, glabrous except axillary tufts

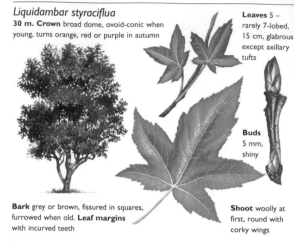

Buds 5 mm, shiny

Bark grey or brown, fissured in squares, furrowed when old. **Leaf margins** with incurved teeth

Shoot woolly at first, round with corky wings

Sweet gum is native to the eastern USA and as far south as Guatemala. The three species in this genus have globose flowers and spiny pendulous fruits, like Plane. Leaves are similar to Maple (pp 154–61) but alternate.

Persian ironwood

Parrotia persica

Flowers before leaves   **Shoot** green-brown, has short stiff hairs, star-shaped

Leaves with 6–9 pairs impressed veins, brown hairs below

Buds downy, brown or black-purple

Flowers only stamens coloured

Bark similar to that of London plane, peels to expose brown or yellow

Leaf margins waved, glossy

Bark smooth, pink-brown or grey-green, exfoliating in large flakes

Persian ironwood, native to the lush forests around the Caspian sea, can grow to 15 m, but is usually a sprawling shrubby tree. It is attractive in autumn when it assumes gold and crimson tints, and is distinguishable by its unusual bark.

Rose family *Rosaceae*

The rose family is a large assemblage of trees, shrubs and herbs, with alternate leaves. The family is characterized by the flowers, which have the sepals, petals and stamens attached to the receptacle margin. The ovary may have one or several carpels and may be superior, above the petals and stamens, or inferior, below them. Four subfamilies are distinguished by fruit.

Two subfamilies, centred on *Rosa*, the Rose, and *Spiraea*, contain only shrubs. *Prunoideae* is defined by having a fruit which is a drupe, a fleshy outer covering around a single bony seed. *Prunus* is the only tree genus, divided into sections based on the flower arrangements.

The subfamily *Maloideae* has a fruit which is a pome, which has 2–5 carpels containing the seeds within a fleshy covering, and includes many tree genera.

Snowy mespilus

Amelanchier lamarckii

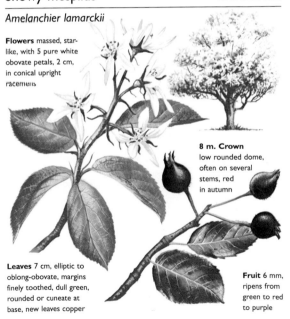

Flowers massed, star-like, with 5 pure white obovate petals, 2 cm, in conical upright racemens

8 m. Crown low rounded dome, often on several stems, red in autumn

Leaves 7 cm, elliptic to oblong-obovate, margins finely toothed, dull green, rounded or cuneate at base, new leaves copper

Fruit 6 mm, ripens from green to red to purple

Snowy mespilus is a small tree or shrub, now naturalized on sandy heaths in Europe, native to eastern North America. The sweet black fruits are edible when they ripen in July. *Amelanchier* is a genus of small trees from North America, Europe and Asia.

Hawthorn, May

Crataegus monogyna

Leaves 10 cm, deeply lobed, with few teeth. **Thorns** to 2.5 cm

Veins pinnate.

Flowers in corymbs of up to 16, appear with leaves in May

15 m. Crown dense. **Bole** short, fluted

Fruit 1 cm, 1-seeded, has persistent calyx, profusely set, ripening September

Shoot purplish, stout.

Buds 2 mm, glabrous, set in pairs at bases of spines

Hawthorn's alternative names, "May" and "Quickthorn", derive from its flowering season and the speed with which it can form hedges. It has pink-flower cultivars such as "Pendula Rosea". Midland hawthorn (*C. laevigata*) is less spiny and has shallowly-lobed leaves, two-seeded haws and veins all pointing forward.

Cockspur thorn

Crataegus crus-galli

Leaves 8 cm

Fruit 1.5 cm, 2-seeded, sometimes persists in winter

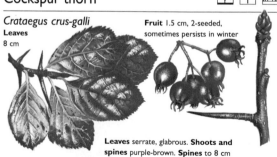

Leaves serrate, glabrous. **Shoots and spines** purple-brown. **Spines** to 8 cm

Native to eastern USA, Cockspur thorn forms a low, rounded tree to 7 m and assumes rich orange tints in autumn. Broadleafed cockspur (*C. x prunifolia*) differs in its wider leaves, dark purple-brown shoots and haws that fall in autumn. Lavalle thorn (*C. x lavallei*) has shiny, blackish-green leaves that are downy below, pubescent shoots with few thorns and 1.5 cm, orange haws.

Medlar

Mespilus germanica

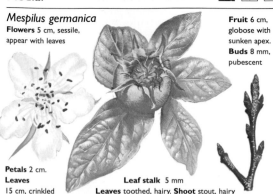

Flowers 5 cm, sessile, appear with leaves

Fruit 6 cm, globose with sunken apex.
Buds 8 mm, pubescent

Petals 2 cm.
Leaves 15 cm, crinkled

Leaf stalk 5 mm
Leaves toothed, hairy. **Shoot** stout, hairy

A low tree closely related to the hawthorns, Medlar is a native of south-eastern Europe but widely cultivated for its large fruit which has persistent calyxes and becomes palatable after it has been bletted or over-ripened. Its single flowers are sessile.

Tree cotoneaster

Cotoneaster frigidus

15 m. Crown wide, rounded, sometimes on several stems, often leaning. **Branches** arch, then level

Bark scaly.
Fruit a pome with 2 nutlets, ripening September, persistent.
Leaves 13 cm, soft, entire, semi-evergreen; some forms more crinkled

Flowers set in dense 6 cm heads, open June

Leaves initially white and hairy on undersides

Fruit 5 mm

Recognizable by its pale bark and its short, often leaning, bole, this Himalayan tree is the tallest of the cotoneasters and reaches 17 m. It usually retains some of its leaves throughout winter. Waterer cotoneaster (*C.* x *watereri*) has narrower, glossy leaves with impressed veins. Some forms may have pale yellow fruit.

Rowans and whitebeams *Sorbus*

This genus produces large corymbs of flowers developing into red, white, pink or russet heads of berries. While the leaves of rowans are pinnate, those of whitebeams are simple and entire; some hybrid taxa such as *S. x thuringiaca* (p 129) have both types.

Rowan

Sorbus aucuparia

Flowers 1 cm, strongly scented, open in May in flat 15 cm corymbs. **Pedicels** densely hairy

Leaves 20 cm, pinnate. **Leaflets** (11–19), serrate with rounded bases. **Rachis** round

Shoot initially hairy, dull grey-purple

Bark shiny, smooth

15 m. Crown ovoid or columnar conic, irregular. **Branches** ascend or arch

Buds 1.7 cm, ovoid, purple with dense grey hairs

Berries 8 mm. **Fruit** ripens scarlet very abruptly in August

'Beissneri' leaflets deeply serrate, yellowish-green

'Asplenifolia' leaflets deeply cut by serrate teeth, lobulate at base

'Beissneri' bark orange or pinkish brown when wet, dull grey when dry

Usually a small tree with a fastigiate habit and a dislike of shady sites, Rowan is native throughout Europe and in western Asia and North Africa either in the open or light woodland. Its other name, "Mountain Ash", refers to the apparent similarity of its foliage to that of Ash (p 182) and its ability to grow up to 2,000 m above sea level. It is often used as a street tree, especially clones such as 'Asplenifolia', 'Beissneri' and 'Xanthocarpa'.

Scarlet rowan

Sorbus commixta 'Embley'

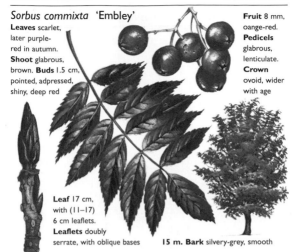

Leaves scarlet, later purple-red in autumn. **Shoot** glabrous, brown. **Buds** 1.5 cm, pointed, adpressed, shiny, deep red

Fruit 8 mm, oange-red. **Pedicels** glabrous, lenticulate. **Crown** ovoid, wider with age

Leaf 17 cm, with (11–17) 6 cm leaflets. **Leaflets** doubly serrate, with oblique bases

15 m. Bark silvery-grey, smooth

A form of the Japanese/Korean rowan, this is often planted as a street tree under the name *S. discolor* which is a much rarer tree with white fruit. Sargent rowan (*S. sargentiana*) has 35 cm leaves with impressed veins and stout shoots with sticky round red buds.

Vilmorin rowan

Sorbus vilmorinii

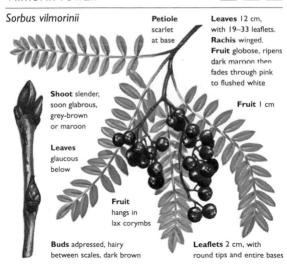

Petiole scarlet at base

Leaves 12 cm, with 19–33 leaflets. **Rachis** winged. **Fruit** globose, ripens dark maroon then fades through pink to flushed white

Shoot slender, soon glabrous, grey-brown or maroon

Leaves glaucous below

Fruit 1 cm

Fruit hangs in lax corymbs

Buds adpressed, hairy between scales, dark brown

Leaflets 2 cm, with round tips and entire bases

Vilmorin rowan is a small tree growing to about 8 m, recognizable by its fern-like foliage and unusual fading fruit. It is a native of western China, as is *Sorbus* 'Joseph Rock', which grows to 10 m, has amber fruits and purple or crimson autumn tints, and slightly longer leaves although with fewer leaflets.

White fruited rowan

Sorbus glabrescens (syn. *Sorbus huphensis*)

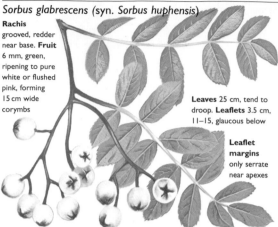

Rachis grooved, redder near base. **Fruit** 6 mm, green, ripening to pure white or flushed pink, forming 15 cm wide corymbs

Leaves 25 cm, tend to droop. **Leaflets** 3.5 cm, 11–15, glaucous below

Leaflet margins only serrate near apexes

A small species of rather gaunt habit, this Chinese tree is noted for its white berries which are often held over winter. Kashmir rowan (*S. cashmiriana*) has ones twice as large and is further identified by pink flowers and leaflets that are fully serrate.

Service tree

Sorbus domestica

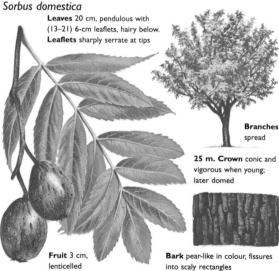

Leaves 20 cm, pendulous with (13–21) 6-cm leaflets, hairy below. **Leaflets** sharply serrate at tips

Branches spread

25 m. Crown conic and vigorous when young; later domed

Fruit 3 cm, lenticelled

Bark pear-like in colour, fissures into scaly rectangles

This Mediterranean species, the largest member of *Sorbus*, reaches 25 m and is sometimes confused with Rowan (p 124). Its apple- or pear-shaped fruit (which is sometimes used for cider-making) is much larger. Larger flowers, resinous buds, a more spreading habit and shredding bark are also keys to identification.

Whitebeam

Sorbus aria

Leaves 8–15 cm.
Petioles 2 cm

20 m. Crown dense. **Branches**
upswept. **Leaf undersides** very downy,
when turned in wind make tree attractive

Flower 1.5 cm, in dense 8 cm corymbs
in May. **Leaf margins** serrate or lobulate

Bark
smooth but
fissured

Buds 1 cm,
conic, tipped
with white hairs.
New leaves
so downy when
open (right) that
appear almost
white. **Shoot**
3 mm thick

Fruit 1.5 cm

S. aria is native to most European chalk and limestone areas and
likes open sites, often on woodland fringes. The whiteness of its
emerging leaves and the persistent pubescence of their undersides
give the species its name. Two forms are widely planted:
'Lutescens' which has very silvery new leaves and 'Decaisneana'
with narrow leaves that are 15 cm long.

Himalayan whitebeam

Sorbus thibetica

Leaves tomentose
below, shiny above

Leaves huge, to 22 × 18 cm

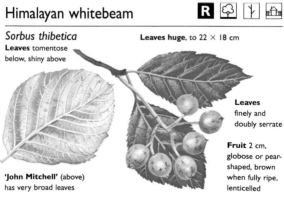

Leaves
finely and
doubly serrate

Fruit 2 cm,
globose or pear-
shaped, brown
when fully ripe,
lenticelled

'John Mitchell' (above)
has very broad leaves

A vigorous, adaptable species with a broad, erect crown reaching
20 m, this whitebeam is noted for its large leaves that remain
silvery below, even when their uppersides have turned russet in
autumn. 'John Mitchell' is a cultivar with very broad leaves.

Wild service tree

Sorbus torminalis

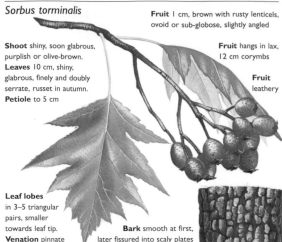

Fruit 1 cm, brown with rusty lenticels, ovoid or sub-globose, slightly angled

Shoot shiny, soon glabrous, purplish or olive-brown.
Leaves 10 cm, shiny, glabrous, finely and doubly serrate, russet in autumn.
Petiole to 5 cm

Fruit hangs in lax, 12 cm corymbs

Fruit leathery

Leaf lobes in 3–5 triangular pairs, smaller towards leaf tip.
Venation pinnate

Bark smooth at first, later fissured into scaly plates

This tree is native to most of Europe but in Britain is mainly restricted to southern clay sites. It usually remains small but occasionally attains 20 m. Its leaves are unique in the *Sorbus* genus and resemble those of some maples.

Service tree of Fontainebleau

Sorbus latifolia

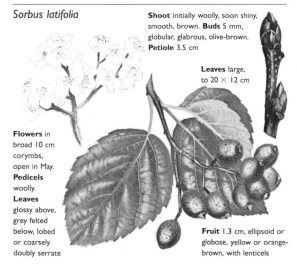

Shoot initially woolly, soon shiny, smooth, brown. **Buds** 5 mm, globular, glabrous, olive-brown.
Petiole 3.5 cm

Leaves large, to 20 × 12 cm

Flowers in broad 10 cm corymbs, open in May.
Pedicels woolly.
Leaves glossy above, grey felted below, lobed or coarsely doubly serrate

Fruit 1.3 cm, ellipsoid or globose, yellow or orange-brown, with lenticels

This tree, an ancient hybrid of Wild service tree and Whitebeam, is one of a number of "microspecies" which are apomyctic, i.e. their seed is produced without cross-fertilization. Amongst the group are *S. bristolensis*, from the Avon Gorge, Bristol, with narrower, cuneate leaves, and *S. anglica*, with shallowly lobed leaves.

Swedish whitebeam

Sorbus intermedia

Buds greenish or red-brown, hairy, 8 mm.
Leaves 12 cm, greyish, white woolly below, darker above

Bark grey or purplish-grey, smooth, fissured

Fruit 1.5 cm, ovoid, glossy green turning to bright scarlet, in bunches of 20

Leaves elliptic, rounded, toothed lobes, cut ⅓ or less to midrib

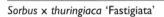

Native to the Baltic countries, Swedish whitebeam is derived from Rowan and Whitebeam. Arran whitebeam (*S. arranensis*) is only native to two glens on the Scottish island of Arran, and has more deeply lobed leaves. Both are good street trees.

Bastard service tree

Sorbus x *thuringiaca* 'Fastigiata'

Shoot grey or purplish, soon glabrous. **Buds** 8 mm, dark red-brown, ovoid or conical, few scales. **Petiole** red

Leaves 11 cm, oblong-obovate, usually with 1–2 (rarely as many as 4) free leaflets, grey woolly below, base cuneate

Lobes decrease in size towards tip

15 m. Crown ovoid, with dense mass of ascending branches. **Bark** smooth dull grey, later becoming shallowly carcked

Leaflets serrate towards tips

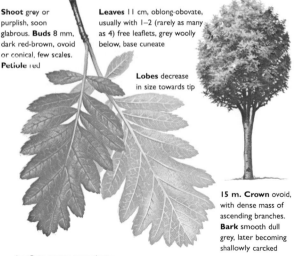

S. thuringianca is a cross between Rowan and Whitebeam which accounts for its partly pinnate leaf. The fruit is scarlet, as in Whitebeam, and carried in lax bunches. It is nearly always encountered as the clone 'Fastigiata' which is a useful street tree. It was first recorded in Thuringia, Germany.

Crab apple

R 🌳 🍃 🏛

Malus sylvestris

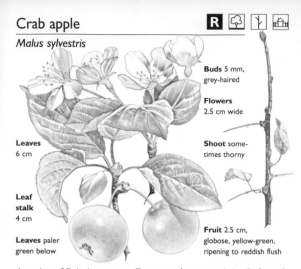

Buds 5 mm, grey-haired

Flowers 2.5 cm wide

Leaves 6 cm

Shoot sometimes thorny

Leaf stalk 4 cm

Leaves paler green below

Fruit 2.5 cm, globose, yellow-green, ripening to reddish flush

A native of Britain, western Europe and western Asia, Crab apple has white flowers, faintly flushed pink, and yields a fruit which, while hard and sour, makes excellent jelly. Crab apple is a parent of Orchard apple (*M. domestica*) which has much pinker flowers, sweeter, softer and larger fruit and hairy shoots and leaves.

Siberian crab

🌳 🍃 🏛

Malus baccata

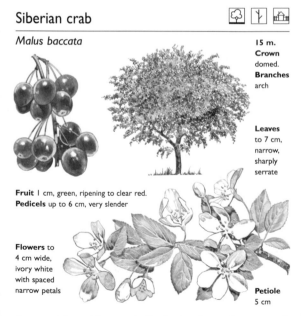

15 m. Crown domed. **Branches** arch

Leaves to 7 cm, narrow, sharply serrate

Fruit 1 cm, green, ripening to clear red.
Pedicels up to 6 cm, very slender

Flowers to 4 cm wide, ivory white with spaced narrow petals

Petiole 5 cm

A tree with a wide natural distribution from Siberia through northern China to the Himalayas, this has fruit which persists through winter when the pointed buds also assist identification. *M. mandshurica* has broader leaves with hairy petioles.

Purple crab

Malus x purpurea

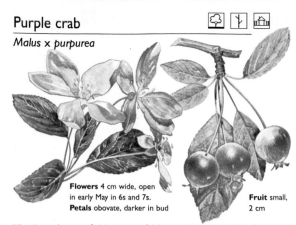

Flowers 4 cm wide, open in early May in 6s and 7s. **Petals** obovate, darker in bud

Fruit small, 2 cm

The 8 cm leaves of this tree unfold purplish red in May but soon become green and glossier above with their main veins purplish below. The form is sparsely branched and reaches 6 m; its cultivars are bigger and more vigorous and include 'Aldenhamensis', 'Eleyi', 'Lemoinei' and 'Profusion'.

Japanese crab

Malus floribunda

Teeth coarse

10 m. Crown dense. **Leaves** to 8 cm, paler and pubescent below, sometimes lobed on vigorous shoots

Flowers 4 cm, red in bud, fading to pink, then whitish, in umbels of 4–7

Fruit 2 cm, ripens yellow or red

Flowers open in May

Shoot hairy, becoming almost glabrous

Japanese crab is most attractive when displaying both its red buds and its pink and white flowers. Chinese crab (*M. spectabilis*) has broader, glossy leaves and large, pink, semi-double flowers. Neither species has indented bases to the fruit.

Hupeh crab

Malus hupehensis

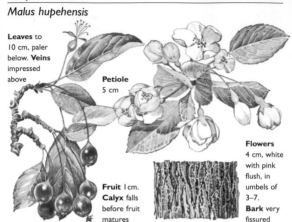

Leaves to 10 cm, paler below. **Veins** impressed above

Petiole 5 cm

Fruit 1 cm. **Calyx** falls before fruit matures

Flowers 4 cm, white with pink flush, in umbels of 3–7. **Bark** very fissured

Hupeh crab has shiny, slightly downy, purple shoots and thorny spur shoots. The leaves can be made into a "red tea". It is very attractive in flower and vigorous, growing to 15 m. Sikkim crab (*M. sikkimensis*) has thornier spur shoots and woolly leaves.

Chonosuki crab

Malus tchonoskii

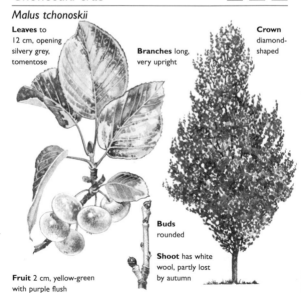

Leaves to 12 cm, opening silvery grey, tomentose

Branches long, very upright

Crown diamond-shaped

Buds rounded

Shoot has white wool, partly lost by autumn

Fruit 2 cm, yellow-green with purple flush

A native of Japan, this makes a good street tree because of its vigorous growth and upright habit. It has brilliant autumn colours. Yunnan crab (*M. yunnanensis*) has yellow-green leaves and 1–2 cm yellow or bright red fruit, speckled white.

Wild pear

Pyrus communis

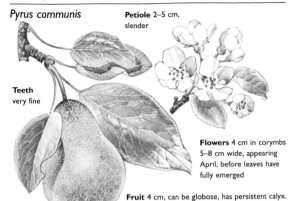

Petiole 2–5 cm, slender

Teeth very fine

Flowers 4 cm in corymbs 5–8 cm wide, appearing April, before leaves have fully emerged

Fruit 4 cm, can be globose, has persistent calyx.
Leaves 8 cm, variable, glossy, paler below

Wild pear is native to most of western Europe but most trees encountered have probably hybridized with selected orchard forms. The crown is narrowly conic at first, becoming tall and domed. 'Beech Hill' is spire-like with erect branches. Chinese pear (*P. calleryana*) has leathery leaves which are hairy on their midrib below.

Willow-leafed pear

Pyrus salicifolia

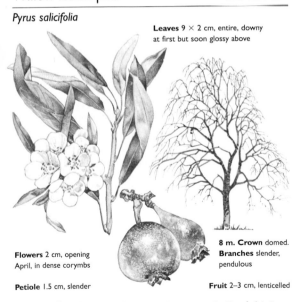

Leaves 9 × 2 cm, entire, downy at first but soon glossy above

Flowers 2 cm, opening April, in dense corymbs

Petiole 1.5 cm, slender

8 m. Crown domed.
Branches slender, pendulous

Fruit 2–3 cm, lenticelled

A native of the Caucasus, this is usually seen as the 'Pendula' clone, which as a young tree has a distinctly weeping habit. Snow pear (*P. nivalis*), from southern Europe, has broader, less glossy leaves and rounded fruit. It reaches 20 m.

Cherries and Plums *Prunus*

The trees in this genus, which also includes Blackthorn, Peach, Apricot and Almond, have fleshy single-seeded fruit which develops from a single ovary. Most species have up to four glands at the junction of their petioles and leaf bases; those without have shoots which are partially green for two or more years.

Wild cherry, Gean

Prunus avium

30 m. Crown open, conic when young

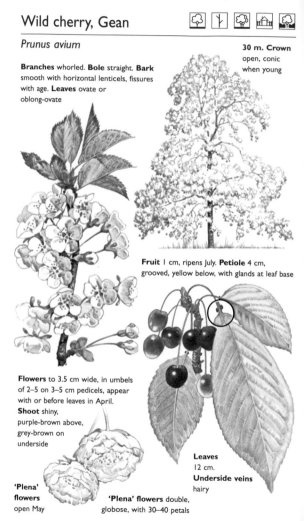

Branches whorled. **Bole** straight. **Bark** smooth with horizontal lenticels, fissures with age. **Leaves** ovate or oblong-ovate

Fruit I cm, ripens July. **Petiole** 4 cm, grooved, yellow below, with glands at leaf base

Flowers to 3.5 cm wide, in umbels of 2–5 on 3–5 cm pedicels, appear with or before leaves in April. **Shoot** shiny, purple-brown above, grey-brown on underside

Leaves 12 cm. **Underside veins** hairy

'Plena' flowers open May

'Plena' flowers double, globose, with 30–40 petals

Wild cherry, also called Gean or Mazard, is native to Europe and western Asia and is striking in flower, when its leaves are bronze, and also in autumn when they turn yellow and red. It is cultivated in areas too cold for apples and is the predominant parent of most domestic fruiting cherries. 'Plena' does not set fruit but its larger flowers persist for up to three weeks. Sour cherry (*P. cerasus*) has a shrubbier, suckering habit, glabrous leaves and tart fruit.

Sargent cherry

Prunus sargentii

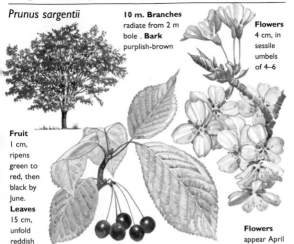

10 m. Branches radiate from 2 m bole . **Bark** purplish-brown

Flowers 4 cm, in sessile umbels of 4–6

Fruit 1 cm, ripens green to red, then black by June. **Leaves** 15 cm, unfold reddish

Flowers appear April

Notable for the brilliant reds and scarlets of its early autumn foliage, Sargent cherry is a large tree that reaches 25 m when growing wild in the mountains of Japan. In cultivation, it is usually grafted to a rootstock of Wild cherry and is much smaller.

Autumn cherry

Prunus x subhirtella 'Autumnalis'

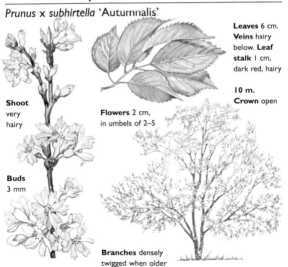

Leaves 6 cm. **Veins** hairy below. **Leaf stalk** 1 cm, dark red, hairy

10 m. Crown open

Shoot very hairy

Flowers 2 cm, in umbels of 2–5

Buds 3 mm

Branches densely twigged when older

This tree has the invaluable asset of flowering intermittently in winter and its semi-double flowers are carried from October to early spring. It is a cultivar of the Japanese Rosebud cherry which is far less common and only carries flowers in April.

Individually identifiable by their various flowers and habits, Japanese cherries comprise about forty small trees which have usually been grafted to a Wild cherry rootstock. Of mixed parentage, they are usually discussed as non-specific cultivars of *Prunus* rather than classified as varieties of *Prunus serrulata*, the species from which most have probably been developed. Collectively, they are sometimes referred to as the "Sato Zakura", which translates as "domestic cherries".

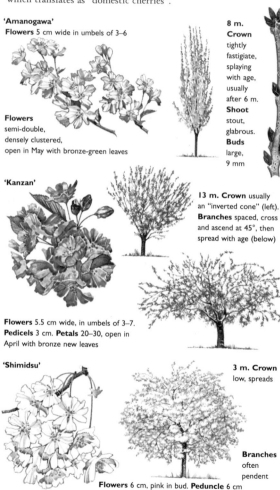

'Amanogawa'
Flowers 5 cm wide in umbels of 3–6

Flowers
semi-double,
densely clustered,
open in May with bronze-green leaves

8 m.
Crown
tightly
fastigiate,
splaying
with age,
usually
after 6 m.
Shoot
stout,
glabrous.
Buds
large,
9 mm

'Kanzan'

13 m. Crown usually
an "inverted cone" (left).
Branches spaced, cross
and ascend at 45°, then
spread with age (below)

Flowers 5.5 cm wide, in umbels of 3–7.
Pedicels 3 cm. **Petals** 20–30, open in
April with bronze new leaves

'Shimidsu'

3 m. Crown
low, spreads

Branches
often
pendent
Flowers 6 cm, pink in bud. **Peduncle** 6 cm

All Sato Zakura have large leaves up to 20 cm long which turn gold or pink in autumn and shoot as shown. The 'Amanogawa' habit instantly identifies it, as do the ascending and crossing branches of the very common 'Kanzan'; no other cherry is so sprawling in old age. The flowers of 'Shimidsu' are notable for their long peduncles.

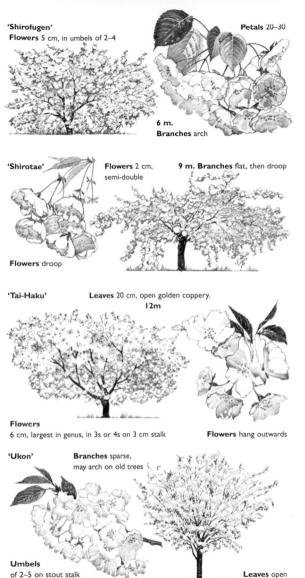

'Shirofugen'
Flowers 5 cm, in umbels of 2–4

Petals 20–30

6 m.
Branches arch

'Shirotae'

Flowers 2 cm, semi-double

9 m. Branches flat, then droop

Flowers droop

'Tai-Haku'

Leaves 20 cm, open golden coppery.
12m

Flowers
6 cm, largest in genus, in 3s or 4s on 3 cm stalk

Flowers hang outwards

'Ukon'

Branches sparse, may arch on old trees

Umbels
of 2–5 on stout stalk

Flowers 5 cm

Leaves open bronze, soon green

'Shirofugen', like 'Shimidsu', flowers very late, in mid-May, but has a vigorous, spreading habit, slightly larger leaves and flowers opening with a pink tinge. The semi-double flowers of 'Shirotae' open a month earlier. 'Ukon' is one of several Japanese cherries with yellow or greenish flowers. 'Tai-Haku' has the largest flowers of any *Prunus* species and is probably closest to the Wild cherry ancestor of the Sato Zakura.

137

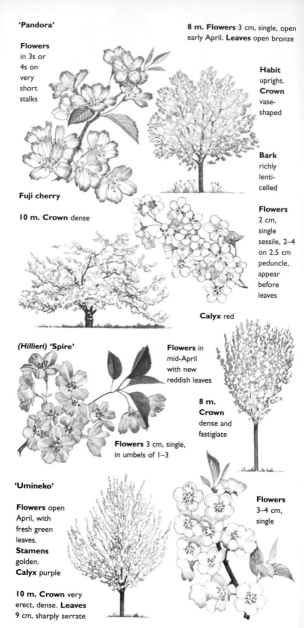

'Pandora'

8 m. Flowers 3 cm, single, open early April. **Leaves** open bronze

Flowers in 3s or 4s on very short stalks

Habit upright. **Crown** vase-shaped

Bark richly lenti-celled

Fuji cherry

10 m. Crown dense

Flowers 2 cm, single sessile, 2–4 on 2.5 cm peduncle, appear before leaves

Calyx red

(Hillieri) 'Spire'

Flowers in mid-April with new reddish leaves

Flowers 3 cm, single, in umbels of 1–3

8 m. Crown dense and fastigiate

'Umineko'

Flowers open April, with fresh green leaves. **Stamens** golden. **Calyx** purple

10 m. Crown very erect, dense. **Leaves** 9 cm, sharply serrate

Flowers 3–4 cm, single

All these cherries have petals set singly and produce small black fruit. Fuji cherry (*P. incisa*) was crossed with Sargent cherry (p 135) to give *P.* 'Hillieri' and 'Spire', (the latter an ideal street tree), and with Oshima cherry (*P. speciosa*) to produce *P.* 'Umineko'. 'Pandora' is another non-specific *Prunus* cultivar (see p 136).

Tibetan cherry

Prunus serrula

Flowers 2 cm, in umbels of 2–4, on 4 cm stalks, appear in May. **Leaves** 12 cm, finely toothed

Bark
glossy, with long bands of lenticels on vigorous trees, peeling and polished

Fruit 5 mm, on 4 cm pedicels. **Leaves** hairy below. **Petiole** 1 cm

Primarily planted for the magnificence of its bark, Tibetan cherry is also noted for its finely serrate willow-like leaves. These are unique among true cherries. *P.* x *schmittii* has a similar but less spectacular bark, an upright habit and pink flowers.

Yoshino cherry

Prunus x *yedoensis*

Leaves to 15 cm, finely pubescent below. **Shoot** slender, hairy

Flowers 3.5 cm, set densely in umbels of 5–6, appear well before leaves, deep pink in bud, soon fade whitish

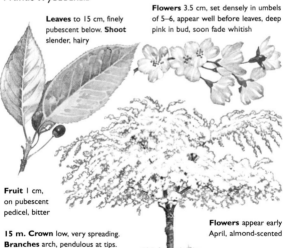

Fruit 1 cm, on pubescent pedicel, bitter

15 m. Crown low, very spreading. **Branches** arch, pendulous at tips. **Bark** grey, darker on large trees

Flowers appear early April, almond-scented

Yoshino is unknown in the wild but is believed to be a hybrid of Rosebud cherry (p 135) and Oshima cherry (*P. speciosa*). It is unusual among Japanese flowering cherries in having densely pubescent leaves, flower stalks and shoots. Its fruit is black.

139

Bird cherry

Prunus padus

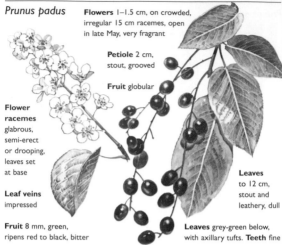

Flowers 1–1.5 cm, on crowded, irregular 15 cm racemes, open in late May, very fragrant

Petiole 2 cm, stout, grooved

Fruit globular

Flower racemes glabrous, semi-erect or drooping, leaves set at base

Leaf veins impressed

Leaves to 12 cm, stout and leathery, dull

Fruit 8 mm, green, ripens red to black, bitter

Leaves grey-green below, with axillary tufts. **Teeth** fine

Bird cherry has a wide distribution from Britain across northern Eurasia to Japan, and is easily recognized when in flower by its semi-erect racemes. Its smooth, dark, bitter-smelling bark was once used to prepare medicinal infusions. This tree has glabrous shoots and pointed and conic 5 mm buds.

Black cherry

Prunus serotina

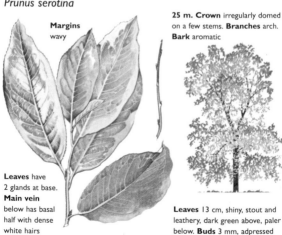

Margins wavy

25 m. Crown irregularly domed on a few stems. **Branches** arch. **Bark** aromatic

Leaves have 2 glands at base. **Main vein** below has basal half with dense white hairs

Leaves 13 cm, shiny, stout and leathery, dark green above, paler below. **Buds** 3 mm, adpressed

Black cherry, one of the largest trees in the genus, grows wild in eastern North America. Its fruit carries persistent calyxes, and its flowers are larger and grow in more erect racemes than those of Bird cherry. The hairy midrib beneath the serrate, glossy leaves and smaller buds distinguish it. Its leaves are held late and fall yellow.

Cherry laurel

Prunus laurocerasus

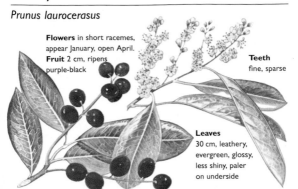

Flowers in short racemes, appear January, open April. **Fruit** 2 cm, ripens purple-black

Teeth fine, sparse

Leaves 30 cm, leathery, evergreen, glossy, less shiny, paler on underside

From south-eastern Europe, this species has large glossy leaves which smell of cyanide, especially when young. It can become a tree of 15 m but is much commoner as a large shrub. It is often called 'Laurel' because of the resemblance of the foliage to the leaves of Bay laurel (see p 106).

Portugal laurel

Prunus lusitanica

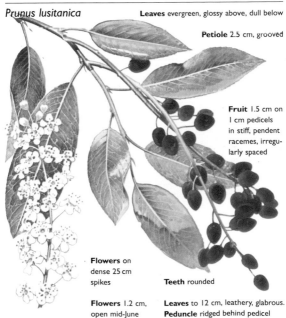

Leaves evergreen, glossy above, dull below

Petiole 2.5 cm, grooved

Fruit 1.5 cm on 1 cm pedicels in stiff, pendent racemes, irregularly spaced

Flowers on dense 25 cm spikes

Teeth rounded

Flowers 1.2 cm, open mid-June

Leaves to 12 cm, leathery, glabrous.
Peduncle ridged behind pedicel

This evergreen species is native to the Iberian peninsula and while usually a shrubby tree of about 8 m may sometimes reach 16 m. Its buds, leaf stalks and shoots are always green. A form with fewer flowers and wider leaves grows in the Azores.

Cherry plum • Purple-leaf plum

Prunus cerasifera • *P. cerasifera* 'Pissardi'

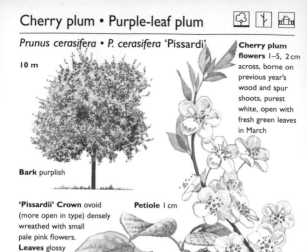

10 m

Cherry plum flowers 1–5, 2 cm across, borne on previous year's wood and spur shoots, purest white, open with fresh green leaves in March

Bark purplish

'Pissardii' Crown ovoid (more open in type) densely wreathed with small pale pink flowers. **Leaves** glossy green. **Veins** impressed

Petiole 1 cm

Fruit red or purple. **Leaves** downy below, toothed, to 7 cm

Fruit 2.5 cm, globose

This attractive tree has an early flowering season, sometimes even in January, or as late as April. The normal green and purple leaf forms are about equally common. Cherry plum is often mistaken for Blackthorn, whose leaves follow its flowers. The edible fruits are not often set in Britain.

Blackthorn, Sloe

Prunus spinosa

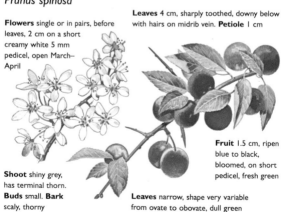

Flowers single or in pairs, before leaves, 2 cm on a short creamy white 5 mm pedicel, open March–April

Leaves 4 cm, sharply toothed, downy below with hairs on midrib vein. **Petiole** 1 cm

Fruit 1.5 cm, ripen blue to black, bloomed, on short pedicel, fresh green

Shoot shiny grey, has terminal thorn. **Buds** small. **Bark** scaly, thorny

Leaves narrow, shape very variable from ovate to obovate, dull green

Blackthorn or Sloe is a small native suckering shrub or small tree to 6 m. In early spring it is a mass of small creamy-white flowers which obliterate the black of the bark and branches. The fruit ripens in October, and is used to flavour gin.

Plum

Prunus domestica

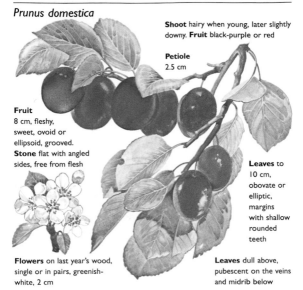

Shoot hairy when young, later slightly downy. **Fruit** black-purple or red

Petiole 2.5 cm

Fruit 8 cm, fleshy, sweet, ovoid or ellipsoid, grooved. **Stone** flat with angled sides, free from flesh

Leaves to 10 cm, obovate or elliptic, margins with shallow rounded teeth

Flowers on last year's wood, single or in pairs, greenish-white, 2 cm

Leaves dull above, pubescent on the veins and midrib below

Plum, a small suckering tree to 10 m, is now thought to be a hybrid between Cherry plum and Blackthorn. Many named varieties are cultivated, and can be grouped into plums and the subsp. *insittia*, which includes the damsons, greengages and Bullace which has downy shoots and rounded fruits.

Apricot

Prunus armeniaca

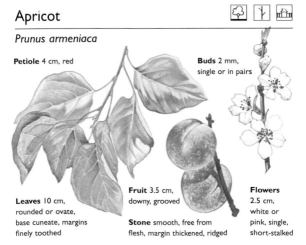

Petiole 4 cm, red

Buds 2 mm, single or in pairs

Leaves 10 cm, rounded or ovate, base cuneate, margins finely toothed

Fruit 3.5 cm, downy, grooved

Stone smooth, free from flesh, margin thickened, ridged

Flowers 2.5 cm, white or pink, single, short-stalked

Apricot makes a small rounded tree to 10 m, and is much cultivated for its delicious orange-red fruit. It does not come from Armenia, as its name suggests, but from northern China. Some cultivars have larger fruit.

Almond

Prunus dulcis

Flowers appear in March, well before leaves, single or in pairs on a short stalk, bright pink; in older trees they appear only slightly in advance of leaves

Leaf usually carries glands at bottom of blade near petiole

Leaves lanceolate, 12 cm, glabrous, finely toothed margins and acuminate tip, "V"-folded near base and along midrib

Petiole 2.5 cm

Fruit 7 cm, velvety; hard thin fleshy coat splits to release seed

Stone, smooth, pitted

Shoot green or purple, **Buds** 1–3 cm

Almond grows wild, with spiny branches, in its native Mediterranean countries. Its early flowering season has endeared it to gardeners, although it is a short-lived tree with a spreading crown to 10 m. Its nuts are used in confectionery.

Peach

Prunus persica

Leaves 18 cm, narrow elliptic, finely serrate, matt green, paler below with raised midrib; do not have basal glands
Buds 2 mm

'Klara Meyer' flowers pure pink, double, 4 cm, singly or in pairs. **Fruit** round, fleshy, 8 cm, stone deeply furrowed, clings to flesh

Shoot green or red-purple. **Shoot** glabrous, angular. **Buds** green and brown

Peach, which only grows to 8 m, is renowned for its juicy fruit, but is also notable for its single pale rose flowers when in blossom. It was introduced from China in the distant past. Nectarine differs only in having a glabrous fruit.

Legume or Pea family
Leguminosae

The Legume or Pea family, comprising several thousand species of trees, shrubs and herbs occurring all over the world, is characterized by pod-like fruits which have a line of seeds along the upper of the two seams. In most familiar species, which belong to the sub-family Papilionoideae, the flowers consist of 10 stamens and 5 petals – a "standard" petal covering the top, two wing petals and two "keel" petals.

The second sub-family, the Caesalpinoideae has different flower forms, often with the front two petals enclosing all the others in bud. The Mimosoideae has tiny flowers clustered in heads or on racemes. All genera except *Cercis* have pinnate or bipinnate leaves.

Judas tree

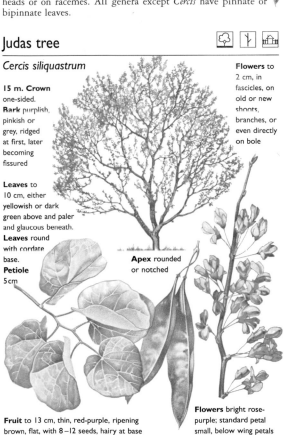

Cercis siliquastrum

15 m. Crown one-sided.
Bark purplish, pinkish or grey, ridged at first, later becoming fissured

Leaves to 10 cm, either yellowish or dark green above and paler and glaucous beneath.
Leaves round with cordate base.
Petiole 5 cm

Apex rounded or notched

Flowers to 2 cm, in fascicles, on old or new shoots, branches, or even directly on bole

Fruit to 13 cm, thin, red-purple, ripening brown, flat, with 8–12 seeds, hairy at base

Flowers bright rose-purple; standard petal small, below wing petals

Judas tree, not, as commonly supposed, the tree upon which Judas Iscariot hung himself, but named after its native Judea, is unique in the Legume family for its orbicular leaves, similar to Katsura (p 115), but distinguishable by its lack of paired buds. Chinese cercis (*C. racemosa*) is the most distinctive of the six other species, with 30–40 rose-pink flowers in a pendulous raceme.

Robinia

Robinia pseudoacacia

Flowers in racemes up to 20 cm long, fragrant, appear mid to late June

Leaf 20 cm, 9–17 leaflets. **Buds** naked, hidden in petiole

30 m. Crown light, open. **Bole** short, fluted. **Bark** smooth, becoming fissured

Shoot ribbed. **Spines** paired, by most buds

Robinia, also called Black locust or False acacia, is native to the eastern USA. Its fruit pods ripen from green through purple to brown and persist during winter. 'Frisia' has golden leaves.

Honey locust

R

Gleditsia triacanthos

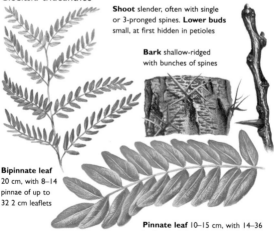

Shoot slender, often with single or 3-pronged spines. **Lower buds** small, at first hidden in petioles

Bark shallow-ridged with bunches of spines

Bipinnate leaf 20 cm, with 8–14 pinnae of up to 32 2 cm leaflets

Pinnate leaf 10–15 cm, with 14–36 leaflets each 2–4 cm, remotely serrate.

This tree often has bipinnate leaves on vigorous shoots and can be distinguished from the closely allied Robinia by its spiny bark, greenish flowers and larger pods. 'Inermis' is often preferred in towns because it lacks spines. 'Sunburst' has rich gold leaves.

Pagoda tree

Sophora japonica

25 m. Crown uneven, low-spreading.
Bark has long, coarse ridges.
Branches very contorted

Shoot
Initially hairy

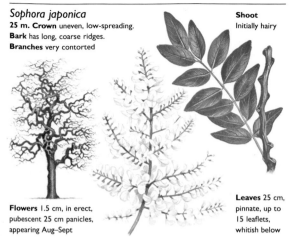

Flowers 1.5 cm, in erect,
pubescent 25 cm panicles,
appearing Aug–Sept

Leaves 25 cm,
pinnate, up to
15 leaflets,
whitish below

The Pagoda tree, although introduced to Europe from Japan, is a
native of China and Korea and differs from Robinia in its pointed,
hairy leaflets and its lack of spines. It produces white, pea-shaped
flowers and pods of up to 8 cm. The Yellow-wood (*Cladrastis lutea*)
has obovate leaflets and a smooth grey bark.

Silver wattle

Acacia dealbata

Leaflets
5 × 1 mm,
finely haired

Leaves 12 cm, bipinnate.
Pinnae in 10–20 pairs,
each with 30–50 pairs
of linear leaflets

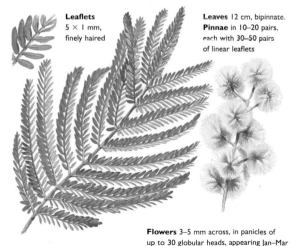

Flowers 3–5 mm across, in panicles of
up to 30 globular heads, appearing Jan–Mar

This Australian tree is only hardy in southern Europe and
although grown in sheltered positions farther north, it cannot
survive harsh winters. It rarely exceeds 15 m. Persian acacia
(*Albizia julibrissin*) has larger, deciduous leaves and pink flowers.

147

Voss laburnum

Laburnum x watereri 'Vossii'

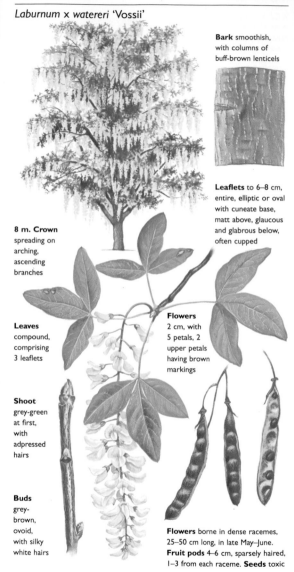

Bark smoothish, with columns of buff-brown lenticels

Leaflets to 6–8 cm, entire, elliptic or oval with cuneate base, matt above, glaucous and glabrous below, often cupped

8 m. Crown spreading on arching, ascending branches

Leaves compound, comprising 3 leaflets

Flowers 2 cm, with 5 petals, 2 upper petals having brown markings

Shoot grey-green at first, with adpressed hairs

Buds grey-brown, ovoid, with silky white hairs

Flowers borne in dense racemes, 25–50 cm long, in late May–June.
Fruit pods 4–6 cm, sparsely haired, 1–3 from each raceme. **Seeds** toxic

One of the showiest of small garden trees, this hybrid of Laburnum (*L. anagyroides*) and Scotch laburnum (*L. alpinum*) combines the longer flowers of the former species with the dense racemes of the latter; both differ from Voss in having silky hairs on their leaf undersides. Hop tree (*Ptelea trifoliata*), in the Rutaceae (p 152), has similarly trifoliate leaves but spotted with oil glands. Its seeds have flat wings like those of elms (pp 106–11).

Quassia family *Simaroubaceae*

Tree of heaven

Ailanthus altissima

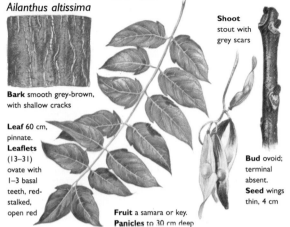

Bark smooth grey-brown, with shallow cracks

Shoot stout with grey scars

Leaf 60 cm, pinnate. **Leaflets** (13–31) ovate with 1–3 basal teeth, red-stalked, open red

Bud ovoid; terminal absent. **Seed wings** thin, 4 cm

Fruit a samara or key. **Panicles** to 30 cm deep

Tree of heaven, with a domed crown to 25 metres, comes from north China. It grows rapidly and tolerates pollution, thriving in city streets and parks. Suckering prodigiously, it can produce leaves up to a metre long when such shoots are cut back.

Box family *Buxaceae*

Box

Buxus sempervirens

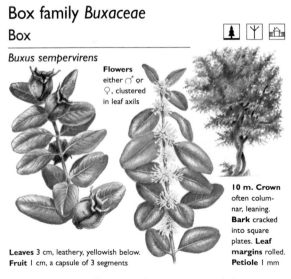

Flowers either ♂ or ♀, clustered in leaf axils

10 m. Crown often columnar, leaning. **Bark** cracked into square plates. **Leaf margins** rolled. **Petiole** 1 mm

Leaves 3 cm, leathery, yellowish below.
Fruit 1 cm, a capsule of 3 segments

Native to some chalky areas of southern England. Box is more common in Mediterranean countries. Its green shoots are square in section and covered in orange hairs while its flowers open in April. It is an ideal tree for hedging and topiary since its small, evergreen leaves are able to withstand repeated clipping. Its hard, heavy wood is much sought-after for engraving.

Cashew family *Anacardiaceae*
Varnish tree

Rhus verniciflua

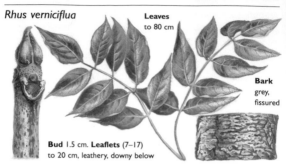

Leaves to 80 cm

Bark grey, fissured

Bud 1.5 cm. **Leaflets** (7–17) to 20 cm, leathery, downy below

The bark of this Asian tree yields a sap used in making furniture lacquer. Potanin sumach (*R. potanini*) has smaller, coarsely toothed leaves and petioles which can enclose the bud.

Stagshorn sumach

Rhus typhina (syn. *Rh. hirsuta*)

Shoot stout, densely covered in short hairs, pithy, has milky sap.

Buds minute, absent as terminals

10 m. Crown low, broad and shrubby. **Bark** thin. **Leaf** 60 cm, has 15–31 leaflets. **Petiole** 8 cm

Leaflets to 12 cm, hairy at first, toothed, magnificent in autumn

Flowers (above) in dense, hairy panicles to 20 cm

Fruit a panicle of densely haired drupes, persistent

The brilliance of its autumn foliage and the curiosity of its crimson "lollipop" fruits remaining well into winter have made this sumach, native to the woods of north-eastern USA, a popular garden tree. Its common name refers to its stout, hairy twigs which resemble the velvety, springtime antlers of stags.

Holly family *Aquifoliaceae*
Holly

Ilex aquifolium

Shoot grooved

Leaf margins undulate. **Petiole** stout, 1 cm. **Buds** small

♂ (and ♀) flower 8 cm, 4-petalled. **Fruit** 6 mm

25 m. Crown pyramidal, dense. **Branches** short. **Bark** smooth. **Leaves** 10 cm, usually prickled but often spineless in upper crown

'Argenteo-marginata' (♂, right) and **'Golden Queen'** (♂) have variegated leaves. **'Bacciflava'** (♀) has very distinctive berries

Highclere holly • *Ilex* x *altaclarensis*

'Camellifolia' cultivar (♀, far left) has leaves with very few prickles. **'Hodginsii'** (♂, left) has broad leaves. **Perny holly** has 3 cm leaves

Holly trees are either male or female and many varied ornamental clones – each with only one sex and each differing in leaf form – have been propagated. Highclere holly is a vigorous hybrid of Holly and Canary holly (*I. perado*) and has large leaves with forward-pointing spines. It, too, has many attractive clones of which 'Hodginsii' is the most common. The Chinese Perny holly (*I. pernyii*) has very small leaves, with 5, rarely 7, spines.

Rue family *Rutaceae*
Korean euodia

Tetradium (Euodia) danielli

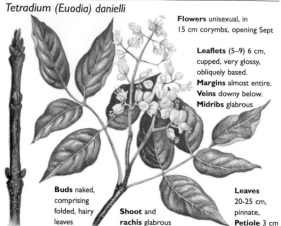

Flowers unisexual, in 15 cm corymbs, opening Sept

Leaflets (5–9) 6 cm, cupped, very glossy, obliquely based.
Margins almost entire.
Veins downy below.
Midribs glabrous

Buds naked, comprising folded, hairy leaves

Shoot and **rachis** glabrous

Leaves 20–25 cm, pinnate, **Petiole** 3 cm

This Korean and Chinese species is valuable for the lateness of its flowering. The Amur cork tree (*Phellodendron amurense*), noted for its thick and coarsely ridged corky bark, has larger leaves with 7–13 leaflets and smaller, greyish buds hidden in the leaf stalk.

Spindle family *Celastraceae*
Spindle tree

Euonymus europaeus

Shoot rounded, with 4 longitudinal ridges. **Leaves** 10 cm, glabrous, matt

Flowers 1 cm, 4-petalled, in cymes of 3–8

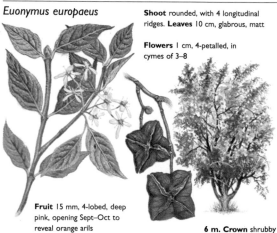

Fruit 15 mm, 4-lobed, deep pink, opening Sept–Oct to reveal orange arils

6 m. Crown shrubby

Native to most of Europe, Spindle is a small tree or shrub renowned for its showy fruit and the attractiveness of its purple-red autumn foliage. Its hard, non-splintering wood was once a useful material for making spindles and other domestic items such as skewers, pegs and knitting needles.

Plane family *Platanaceae*

While it has few botanical affiliations with the Aceraceae (pp 154–65), the leaves of this family are easily mistaken for those of maples. This is reflected in the specific names of two maples – *platonoides* (p 154) and *pseudoplatanus* (p 155) – and in a synonym of London plane *acerifolia*. Planes, however, always have *alternate* leaves.

Oriental plane

R ⬚ ⬚ ⬚

Platanus orientalis

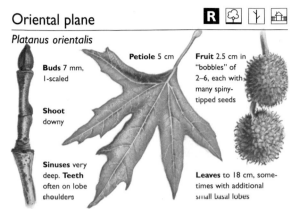

Buds 7 mm, 1-scaled

Shoot downy

Petiole 5 cm

Fruit 2.5 cm in "bobbles" of 2–6, each with many spiny-tipped seeds

Sinuses very deep. **Teeth** often on lobe shoulders

Leaves to 18 cm, sometimes with additional small basal lobes

This species from the eastern Mediterranean can grow 30 metres high and is used as a shade tree in many southern European villages. Its shortish bole can achieve a girth as large as 13 metres.

London plane

⬚ ⬚ ⬚

Platanus x *hispanica* (syn. *P.* x *acerifolia*)

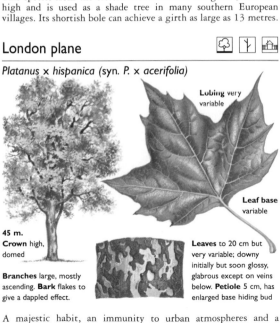

Lobing very variable

Leaf base variable

45 m. Crown high, domed

Branches large, mostly ascending. **Bark** flakes to give a dappled effect.

Leaves to 20 cm but very variable; downy initially but soon glossy, glabrous except on veins below. **Petiole** 5 cm, has enlarged base hiding bud

A majestic habit, an immunity to urban atmospheres and a resistance to barbaric and unsightly pollarding have contributed to this tree's popularity and its success was confirmed last century when it became widely planted in London streets. It is a hybrid of *P. orientalis* and American plane (*P. occidentalis*) which has more shallowly lobed leaves and single, rarely paired, fruit.

153

Maple family *Aceraceae*

Maples are noted for the rich autumnal tints of their leaves which are usually palmately lobed and always set in opposite pairs. Small green or yellow flowers appear in corymbs, racemes or panicles and are normally bisexual. Distinctive samaras (fruit keys) consist of paired seeds (nutlets) set in flat, membranous wings to facilitate wind dispersal.

Norway maple

Acer platanoides

Flowers open early Apr, before lvs in erect corymbs of 20–30. **Petals** 8 mm wide. **Buds** 1 cm tall, red-purple. **Shoot** stout, hairless dark brown

25 m. **Crown** broad-domed, densely leaved. **Bole** short. **Bark** grey-brown, finely ridged

Leaf 12 × 15 cm, cordate. 2–6 coarse teeth per lobe, edges of central lobes parallel. **Blade** paler (below). **Leaf stalk** long, 15 cm, with milky sap distinguishing it from similar maples

Samara nutlets flat. **Wings** each 3–5 cm, almost horizontal

'Schwedleri' open pink-red. Green by summer then purple in autumn

'Drummon-dii' cv has small leaves with white or cream variegation

Native to northern and central Europe, Norway maple is most attractive in April when its flowers open and in autumn when its foliage turns deep yellow. This tree is suited to urban sites and a wide range of cultivars is available: 'Crimson King' and 'Goldsworth Purple' have deep red-purplish leaves throughout summer.

Sycamore

Acer pseudoplatanus

Shoot green-brown. **Buds** ovoid, 1 cm, green, red margins. **Flowers** 50–100, hanging in dense, 12 cm panicles

Samara wings each 3 cm set at 90°

35 m. Crown broad. **Branches** billow. **Bark** scaly, light grey-brown; silver, smooth on young trees. Sycamores often grown for hard, close-grained timber and to act as windbreaks

Leaf to 18 × 26 cm on young trees, more often 15 × 20 cm. 5 lobes, more rarely 3–7. **Teeth** coarse. **Blade** underside glaucous. **Veins** net-like. **Leaf stalk** reddish

'Erectum' (1) has fastigiate brs. Lvs of 'Purpureum' (2) are matt green with purple undersides

'Brilliantissimum' leaf (1) opens shrimp-pink, turning through yellow to dark green. 'Leopoldii' (2) can have leaves stained yellowish-pink. 'Worleei' cv leaf (3) opens in gold and yellow, fading to green-yellow

A wide tolerance of different sites and a facility to germinate, which can make it a rapacious weed, have enabled the Sycamore to colonize most of Britain. Van Volxem maple (*A. velutinum*) has larger leaves and upright flower panicles. Devil's horn maple (*A. diabolicum*) has ciliate, pubescently veined leaves.

Field maple

Acer campestre

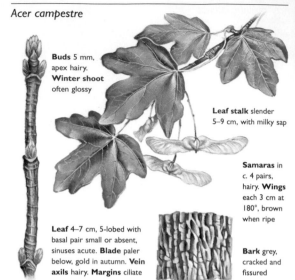

Buds 5 mm, apex hairy. **Winter shoot** often glossy

Leaf stalk slender 5–9 cm, with milky sap

Samaras in c. 4 pairs, hairy. **Wings** each 3 cm at 180°, brown when ripe

Leaf 4–7 cm, 5-lobed with basal pair small or absent, sinuses acute. **Blade** paler below, gold in autumn. **Vein axils** hairy. **Margins** ciliate

Bark grey, cracked and fissured

Field maple is a common hedgerow tree throughout Europe and the only maple native to Britain, where it is common in the south. The Miyabe maple (*A. miyabei*), from Japan, has larger, paler leaves cut less than halfway to the leaf base and a leaf stalk which clasps the shoot very strongly, almost hiding the bud.

Italian maple

Acer opalus

Flowers appear in April before lvs, in pendulous corymbs. **Fruit** in bunches 8–16. **Wings** each 2.5 cm, acutely angled

Winter twig glabrous with pale lenticels

Leaf 12 cm, 3- or 5-lobed. **Teeth** coarse, irregular. **Veins** impressed. **Blade** underside glaucous, hairy. **Leaf stalk** 10 cm with watery sap

Italian maple, also found in France and Spain, is a small tree reaching 15 m. Heldreich maple (*A. heldreichii*) has deep, narrow leaf sinuses – Trauvetter's maple (*A. trauvetteri*) has deep, wide ones. Both these species have *erect* flower panicles.

Caucasian maple

Acer cappadocium

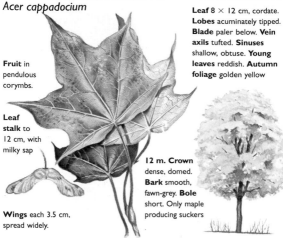

Leaf 8 × 12 cm, cordate. **Lobes** acuminately tipped. **Blade** paler below. **Vein axils** tufted. **Sinuses** shallow, obtuse. **Young leaves** reddish. **Autumn foliage** golden yellow

Fruit in pendulous corymbs.

Leaf stalk to 12 cm, with milky sap

12 m. Crown dense, domed. **Bark** smooth, fawn-grey. **Bole** short. Only maple producing suckers

Wings each 3.5 cm, spread widely.

Native to Asia Minor and the Caucasus, with varieties in the Himalayas and China, Caucasian maple has a particularly beautiful, golden autumn colour. Its cultivar 'Aurum' has pale yellow-green leaves while those of 'Rubrum' have their new growth tinged deep red. Thunberg maple (*A. mono*) has similar leaves but is recognizable by its grey-brown shoots.

Lobel maple

Acer lobelii

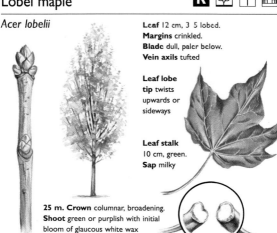

Leaf 12 cm, 3–5 lobed. **Margins** crinkled. **Blade** dull, paler below. **Vein axils** tufted

Leaf lobe tip twists upwards or sideways

Leaf stalk 10 cm, green. **Sap** milky

25 m. Crown columnar, broadening. **Shoot** green or purplish with initial bloom of glaucous white wax

With similarly lobed, toothless leaves and shoots which stay green for several years, Lobel maple can easily be confused with *A. cappadocium* but is ultimately differentiated from it by the twisted tips and wrinkled margins of its leaves and bloomed shoots. It grows wild in the mountain woodlands of southern Italy.

Oregon maple

Acer macrophyllum

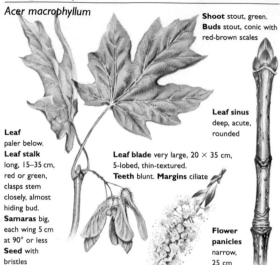

Shoot stout, green.
Buds stout, conic with red-brown scales

Leaf sinus deep, acute, rounded

Leaf paler below.
Leaf stalk long, 15–35 cm, red or green, clasps stem closely, almost hiding bud.
Samaras big, each wing 5 cm at 90° or less
Seed with bristles

Leaf blade very large, 20 × 35 cm, 5-lobed, thin-textured.
Teeth blunt. **Margins** ciliate

Flower panicles narrow, 25 cm

This North American Coast species grows quickly into a majestic tree of 20–30 m with a tall, domed crown of ascending, arched branches. Oregon is the only maple with both milky sap *and* hanging panicles and its large leaves and clasping leaf stalks will readily confirm this identification.

Sugar maple

Acer saccharum

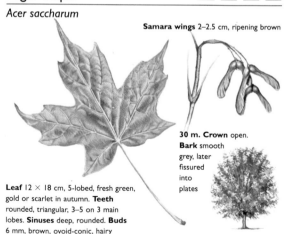

Samara wings 2–2.5 cm, ripening brown

30 m. Crown open.
Bark smooth grey, later fissured into plates

Leaf 12 × 18 cm, 5-lobed, fresh green, gold or scarlet in autumn. **Teeth** rounded, triangular, 3–5 on 3 main lobes. **Sinuses** deep, rounded. **Buds** 6 mm, brown, ovoid-conic, hairy

In its native range stretching from eastern Canada to Texas, this is the tree tapped for maple syrup. Its leaf is not dissimilar to that of Norway maple (p 154) but it has a water sap. Black maple (*A. nigrum*) has darker, duller, yellow-veined leaves which are cupped and three-lobed. Its bark is ridged.

Silver maple

Acer saccharinum

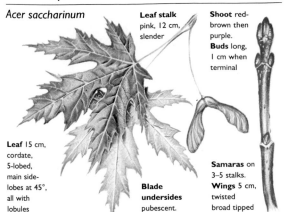

Leaf stalk pink, 12 cm, slender

Shoot red-brown then purple.
Buds long, 1 cm when terminal

Leaf 15 cm, cordate, 5-lobed, main side-lobes at 45°, all with lobules

Blade undersides pubescent.

Samaras on 3–5 stalks.
Wings 5 cm, twisted broad tipped

Silver maple is native to eastern North America south of Quebec and grows to some 30 m with a tall, raggedly domed crown and a smooth, silver bark. In early March its maroon flowers, opening before the leaves, enliven the tree; in autumn its foliage assumes spectacular hues of yellow, gold or red.

Red maple

Acer rubrum

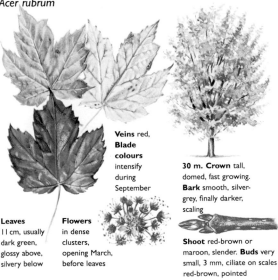

Veins red, Blade colours intensify during September

30 m. Crown tall, domed, fast growing.
Bark smooth, silver-grey, finally darker, scaling

Leaves 11 cm, usually dark green, glossy above, silvery below

Flowers in dense clusters, opening March, before leaves

Shoot red-brown or maroon, slender. **Buds** very small, 3 mm, ciliate on scales red-brown, pointed

This North American tree is aptly named since its flowers, fruits, shoots and autumn tints are all red or reddish; its leaf undersides and bark are silver. It is closely related to Silver maple, often growing near it, but has smaller, less deeply lobed leaves.

159

Japanese maple

Acer palmatum

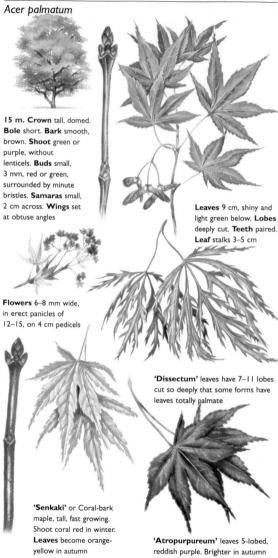

15 m. Crown tall, domed. **Bole** short. **Bark** smooth, brown. **Shoot** green or purple, without lenticels. **Buds** small, 3 mm, red or green, surrounded by minute bristles. **Samaras** small, 2 cm across. **Wings** set at obtuse angles

Leaves 9 cm, shiny and light green below. **Lobes** deeply cut. **Teeth** paired. **Leaf** stalks 3–5 cm

Flowers 6–8 mm wide, in erect panicles of 12–15, on 4 cm pedicels

'Dissectum' leaves have 7–11 lobes cut so deeply that some forms have leaves totally palmate

'Senkaki' or Coral-bark maple, tall, fast growing. Shoot coral red in winter. **Leaves** become orange-yellow in autumn

'Atropurpureum' leaves 5-lobed, reddish purple. Brighter in autumn

Japanese maple is a small, bushy tree. While its leaves turn brilliant shades in autumn, it can be equally attractive in spring, when its purple flowers contrast strongly with its fresh green leaves. Of the enormous range of its cultivars, the most spectacular is 'Senkaki' and the most popular, 'Atropurpureum'. Oliver maple (*A. oliverianum*), from central China, has stiffer and glossier leaves which are five-lobed and minutely serrate. Their undersides are often pubescent.

Full-moon maple

Acer japonicum

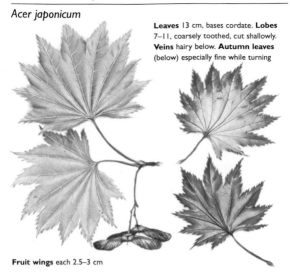

Leaves 13 cm, bases cordate. **Lobes** 7–11, coarsely toothed, cut shallowly. **Veins** hairy below. **Autumn leaves** (below) especially fine while turning

Fruit wings each 2.5–3 cm

This native of Japan derives its name from its orbicular leaves. It is represented in gardens by: 'Vitifolium' with leaves up to 15 cm offering fine autumn colour; 'Aureum', smaller, with golden yellow foliage and may be a hybrid of *A. shirasawanum*.

David maple

Acer davidii

Leaf blades ovate with pointed tips but very varied as 'George Forrest' (right), 'Ernest Wilson' (below).

Margins unevenly serrate. **Veins** parallel, main one red with minute axil tufts

Bark olive green with white or green "snaking" stripes. **Branches** ascend steeply. **Shoot** maroon or dark green-red, later striped white. **Buds** 1 cm

This is the most common of the snake-bark maples, which have distinctive barks with white or greenish stripes and flowers in long, dense racemes. It has a wide natural distribution in China and as a species is extremely variable. One form, 'Ernest Wilson', has a lower, rounded habit and yellower, narrower leaves folded at the base of their main vein.

Kyushu maple

Acer capillipes

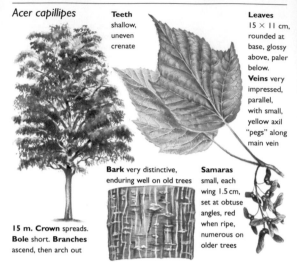

Teeth shallow, uneven crenate

Leaves 15 × 11 cm, rounded at base, glossy above, paler below. **Veins** very impressed, parallel, with small, yellow axil "pegs" along main vein

Bark very distinctive, enduring well on old trees

Samaras small, each wing 1.5 cm, set at obtuse angles, red when ripe, numerous on older trees

15 m. Crown spreads. **Bole** short. **Branches** ascend, then arch out

This Japanese maple is the only snake-bark whose leaves have small forward-pointing side lobes, impressed veins and yellowish axil "pegs". Its autumn colours and red shoots and buds give it the alternative name of "Red snake-bark maple".

Moosewood

Acer pensylvanicum

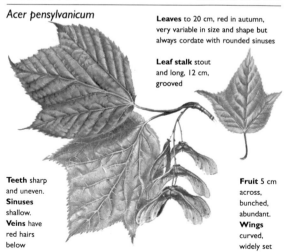

Leaves to 20 cm, red in autumn, very variable in size and shape but always cordate with rounded sinuses

Leaf stalk stout and long, 12 cm, grooved

Teeth sharp and uneven. **Sinuses** shallow. **Veins** have red hairs below

Fruit 5 cm across, bunched, abundant. **Wings** curved, widely set

Moosewood, from eastern North America, is the only snake-bark not indigenous to eastern Asia. Honshu maple (*A. rufinerve*), from Japan, has smaller leaves with rufous, pubescent veins, buds bloomed white and small, round nutlets. Hers' maple (*A. hersii*) has matt leaves, larger fruit and no red colouring.

Montpelier maple

R

Acer monspessulanum

Buds small, 3 mm, ovoid.
Shoot slender, slightly glossy.
Flowers open in June
(with or before leaves) in small,
erect panicles that are 5 cm wide

Samara
wings small,
each 1.2 cm, set
almost parallel
or overlapping

Leaf 4 × 7 cm, cordate,
usually entire. **Blade underside**
glaucous with some axil tufts near
base. **Leaf stalk** 4 cm, slender, pink

This maple has a wide natural range from Mediterranean Spain and north Africa to Iran where it is often used for hedging, rarely reaching a maximum height of 15 m. Cretan maple (*A. sempervirens*) is almost evergreen and has small, stiff, variable leaves, which may be unlobed or have three rounded lobes.

Amur maple

R

Acer ginnala

10 m. Crown round domed. **Branches** slender.

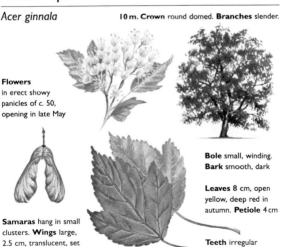

Flowers
in erect showy
panicles of c. 50,
opening in late May

Bole small, winding.
Bark smooth, dark

Leaves 8 cm, open
yellow, deep red in
autumn. **Petiole** 4 cm

Samaras hang in small
clusters. **Wings** large,
2.5 cm, translucent, set
almost parallel

Teeth irregular

Amur maple, from north-east Asia, is a small shrubby tree which shows its early autumn crimson for a brief period in September. Trident maple (*A. buergerianum*) has three-lobed leaves, the lobes pointing directly forward in the manner of Neptune's trident. These leaves have silvery undersides.

Paperbark maple

Acer griseum

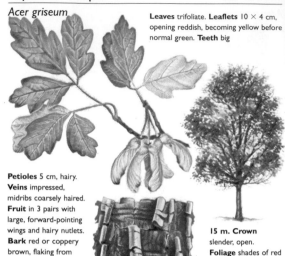

Leaves trifoliate. **Leaflets** 10 × 4 cm, opening reddish, becoming yellow before normal green. **Teeth** big

Petioles 5 cm, hairy. **Veins** impressed, midribs coarsely haired. **Fruit** in 3 pairs with large, forward-pointing wings and hairy nutlets. **Bark** red or coppery brown, flaking from both bole and branches

15 m. **Crown** slender, open. **Foliage** shades of red and orange in autumn

Paperbark maple, from central China, is planted for its exquisite but fleeting autumn tints and the permanent beauty of its bark. Chosen maple (*A. triflorum*), whose name derives from the Japanese for Korea, has a rough, grey-brown bark. Rock maple (*A. pentaphyllum*) has digitate leaves, glaucous beneath.

Nikko maple

Acer maximowiczianum (syn. Acer nikoense)

Leaflet undersides pubescent. **Leaf stalks** 7 cm, thick, densely haired. **Samara wings** in 3 pairs, broad, 2.5 cm long, glabrous, set at angle of 90° or more. **Nutlets** very hairy

Leaves trifoliate, opening in April. **Leaflets** 10 × 3.5 cm, leathery; side ones subsessile, obliquely based. **Teeth** very small

Bark smooth, initially grey with greenish tinge, becoming pink-grey with fine red speckles

Nikko maple, native to Japan and central China, has lively autumn foliage although its bark cannot compare with that of Paperback maple. Manchurian maple (*A. mandschuricum*) has a similar bark to Nikko but saw-toothed leaves with long stalks.

Box elder

Acer negundo

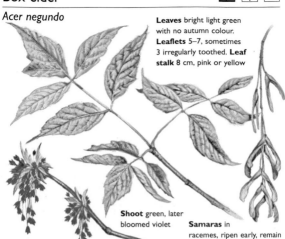

Leaves bright light green with no autumn colour. **Leaflets** 5–7, sometimes 3 irregularly toothed. **Leaf stalk** 8 cm, pink or yellow

Shoot green, later bloomed violet

♂ **flowers** set in pendulous clusters of 12–16

Samaras in racemes, ripen early, remain after leaf fall. **Wings** 2 cm, set acutely, incurved.

Possibly overplanted, Box elder rarely produces a fine specimen; its cultivar 'Variegatum' produces both fruit and leaves that are variegated white. Henry maple (*A. henryi*) is a Chinese species with red autumn foliage, pink-red leaf stalks and bright green, glossy shoots.

Pittosporum family *Pittosporaceae*

Pittosporum

Pittosporum tenuifolium

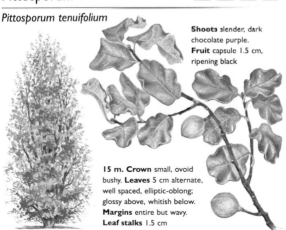

Shoots slender, dark chocolate purple. **Fruit** capsule 1.5 cm, ripening black

15 m. Crown small, ovoid bushy. **Leaves** 5 cm alternate, well spaced, elliptic-oblong; glossy above, whitish below. **Margins** entire but wavy. **Leaf stalks** 1.5 cm

This pittosporum family comes mainly from Australasia, south-east Asia and South Africa although one species is native to Madeira. Pittosporum itself is native to both islands of New Zealand and is noticeable for its fragrant flowers.

Horse chestnut family *Hippocastanaceae*

This small family, named after the resemblance of its fruit to that of *Castanea* (p 105), is dominated by the *Aesculus* genus. Opposite, digitately compound leaves, showy and erect flower panicles and large "conker" seeds are identifying features.

Horse chestnut

Aesculus hippocastanum

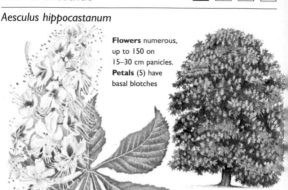

Flowers numerous, up to 150 on 15–30 cm panicles. **Petals** (5) have basal blotches

40 m. Crown tall, spreading, dense. **Branches** upswept, sometimes layering. **Buds** 2.5 cm. **Shoot** stout. **Leaf** scars horseshoe shaped

Leaflets (5–7) 10–25 cm, sessile, unevenly serrate **Fruit** 5 cm

This species provides the ammunition for conkers which was once played with snail shells (conches). Japanese horse chestnut (*A. turbinata*) also has sticky buds *and* sessile leaflets but the latter are evenly toothed and can be up to 40 cm long.

Red horse chestnut

Aesculus × carnea

Buds not sticky. **Flowers** in 12–20 cm panicles, opening May; 'Briottii' flowers are deeper red

Bark rough, not scaly at base. **Bole** often cankered

This hybrid is smaller than its Horse chestnut parent while its buds resemble those of its other parent, the American Red buckeye (*A. pavia*) which has the same red inflorescences.

Indian horse chestnut

Aesculus indica

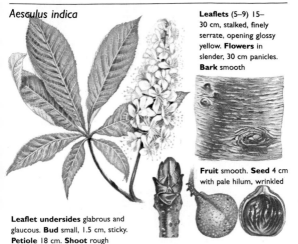

Leaflets (5–9) 15–30 cm, stalked, finely serrate, opening glossy yellow. **Flowers** in slender, 30 cm panicles. **Bark** smooth

Fruit smooth. **Seed** 4 cm with pale hilum, wrinkled

Leaflet undersides glabrous and glaucous. **Bud** small, 1.5 cm, sticky. **Petiole** 18 cm. **Shoot** rough

This majestic native of the Himalayas flowers and fruits 6 weeks after *A. hippocastanum* and is the most common of those *Aesculus* species with 4-petalled flowers and resinous buds. Another is California buckeye (*A. californica*) which has pear-shaped fruit, smaller, sessile leaflets and flat petioles.

Yellow buckeye

Aesculus flava

20 m. Crown narrow with fine autumn yellows and orange-reds. **Branches** small, pendulous and twisting. **Bole** straight. **Bark** grey- or red-brown, smooth becoming scaly

Leaves have 5–7 leaflets with impressed veins. **Flowers** 4 cm, dense, sometimes pink, on 10–15 cm panicles. **Petals** (4) forward-pointing

Leaflet margins finely serrate

Leaflet 15 cm, glabrous, sometimes downy below, on 1.5 cm stalk. **Fruit** 6 cm, smooth, 2-seeded

Buckeyes, whose name arose when their hila (pale, basal seed scars) were likened to the eyes of deer, are native to the eastern USA. They have non-sticky buds. Yellow buckeye presents the best of their autumn tints. The doubly serrate leaves of Sunrise buckeye (*A. neglecta* 'Erythroblastos') open pink-red.

Lime family *Tiliaceae*

Limes have large, toothed, heart-shaped leaves, flowers that hang in cymes and large distinctive bracts attached for half their length to the flower stalk. The fruit is dry and nutty.

Large-leaved lime

Tilia platyphyllos

Leaf margins have crenate and serrate teeth. **Shoot** hairy. **Buds** red, 3-scaled

Leaf stalk 5 cm, hairy. **Flowers** (3–6) 12 mm

Bract large, 12 cm. **Fruit** 1 cm, round, densely pubescent, 5-ribbed, in 3s

Leaves 16 cm, but variable – other lime leaves often bigger. **Blade** hairy above, densely to below on vein midrib and axils

The Large-leaved lime is native to most of Europe (including parts of Britain) and has a narrow crown with branches that ascend steeply. Its bark is grey and fissured; shoots at the foot of the bole are rare. American lime (*T. americana*) has larger leaves which are coarsely toothed, almost glabrous and paler below.

Small-leaved lime

Tilia cordata

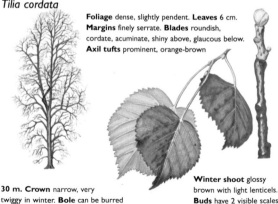

Foliage dense, slightly pendent. **Leaves** 6 cm. **Margins** finely serrate. **Blades** roundish, cordate, acuminate, shiny above, glaucous below. **Axil tufts** prominent, orange-brown

30 m. Crown narrow, very twiggy in winter. **Bole** can be burred

Winter shoot glossy brown with light lenticels. **Buds** have 2 visible scales

This species of lime is recognizable by the size of its roundish leaves and its flowers, which spread irregularly and do not hang. Mongolian lime (*T. mongolica*) is often planted where a smaller tree is required. Its leaves have large, coarse, triangular teeth which almost become lobes.

European lime

Tilia x europaea (syn. T x vulgaris)

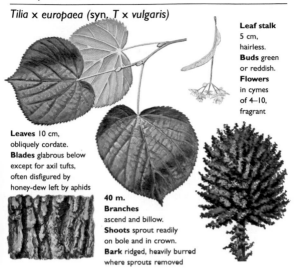

Leaf stalk 5 cm, hairless. **Buds** green or reddish. **Flowers** in cymes of 4–10, fragrant

Leaves 10 cm, obliquely cordate. **Blades** glabrous below except for axil tufts, often disfigured by honey-dew left by aphids

40 m. Branches ascend and billow. **Shoots** sprout readily on bole and in crown. **Bark** ridged, heavily burred where sprouts removed

Often the largest broadleaf in an area, the European lime is a natural hybrid of the Large- and Small-leaved species and its apparent ubiquity as a park and street tree has been attributed to seventeenth-century Dutch horticulturists who found it easier to propagate than its parents. It is often pollarded.

Caucasian lime

Tilia x euchlora

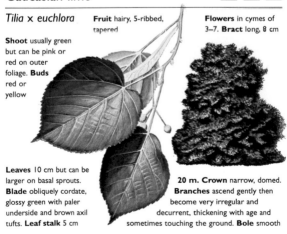

Fruit hairy, 5-ribbed, tapered

Flowers in cymes of 3–7. **Bract** long, 8 cm

Shoot usually green but can be pink or red on outer foliage. **Buds** red or yellow

Leaves 10 cm but can be larger on basal sprouts. **Blade** obliquely cordate, glossy green with paler underside and brown axil tufts. **Leaf stalk** 5 cm

20 m. Crown narrow, domed. **Branches** ascend gently then become very irregular and decurrent, thickening with age and sometimes touching the ground. **Bole** smooth

Caucasian lime has uncertain origins and may be a cross between the Small-leaved lime and the rare *T. dasystyla*, also from the Caucasus. Its agreeable foliage and immunity to aphids make it more suitable for streets than European lime although its lower branches eventually become far too decurrent for such sites.

Silver lime

Tilia tomentosa

Leaf blades 12 × 10 cm, rounded, obliquely cordate, densely pubescent below. **Buds** 6–8 mm. **Shoot** remains pubescent

Leaf stalk to 5 cm, less than half blade length

Bract 9 × 2 cm
Flower buds (7–10) open late July

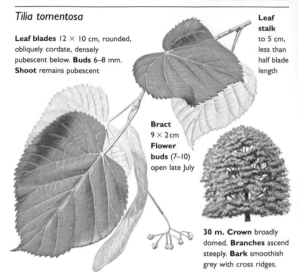

30 m. Crown broadly domed. **Branches** ascend steeply. **Bark** smoothish grey with cross ridges.

Silver lime displays an attractive habit, especially when its pubescent leaves are ruffled by wind. It is a native of the Balkans. Oliver lime (*T. oliveri*), from China, has larger, evenly cordate leaves and glabrous shoots.

Pendent silver lime

Tilia 'Petiolaris'

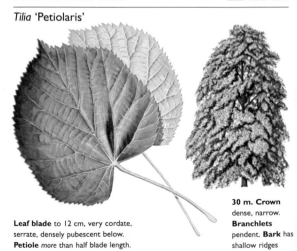

30 m. Crown dense, narrow. **Branchlets** pendent. **Bark** has shallow ridges

Leaf blade to 12 cm, very cordate, serrate, densely pubescent below. **Petiole** more than half blade length.

Usually grafted on to *T. europaea* (p 169), producing an unsightly change in bark texture at a height of some 2 m, this tree hybridizes with *T. americana* (p 168) to produce Von Moltke lime (*T. x moltkei*) whose larger leaves are lightly pubescent below.

Soapberry family *Sapindaceae*
Pride of India

Koelreuteria paniculata

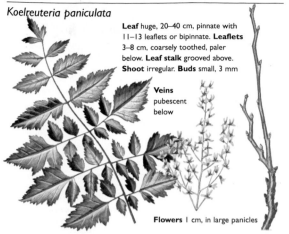

Leaf huge, 20–40 cm, pinnate with 11–13 leaflets or bipinnate. **Leaflets** 3–8 cm, coarsely toothed, paler below. **Leaf stalk** grooved above. **Shoot** irregular. **Buds** small, 3 mm

Veins pubescent below

Flowers 1 cm, in large panicles

A native of Japan and China, this tree has few associations with India. It reaches a maximum height of 15 m, has a widespreading crown and is distinguished by its decurrent leaflets, showy flowers and bladder-like fruit. It turns yellow in autumn.

Euchryphia family *Eucryphiaceae*
Nymans eucryphia

Eucryphia x nymansensis 'Nymansay'

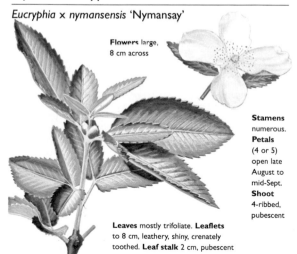

Flowers large, 8 cm across

Stamens numerous. **Petals** (4 or 5) open late August to mid-Sept. **Shoot** 4-ribbed, pubescent

Leaves mostly trifoliate. **Leaflets** to 8 cm, leathery, shiny, crenately toothed. **Leaf stalk** 2 cm, pubescent

An attractive, columnar evergreen and the more valuable for being late-flowering, this tree is a cross between two Chilean species of eucryphia. Rostrevor eucryphia (*E. x intermedia*) has smaller flowers and darker leaves that are glaucous below.

171

Tea family *Theaceae*
Deciduous camellia

Stewartia pseudocamellia

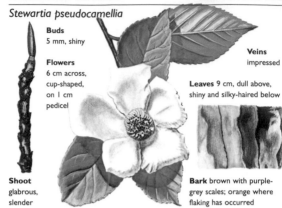

Buds 5 mm, shiny

Flowers 6 cm across, cup-shaped, on 1 cm pedicel

Veins impressed

Leaves 9 cm, dull above, shiny and silky-haired below

Shoot glabrous, slender

Bark brown with purple-grey scales; orange where flaking has occurred

Deciduous camellia, a small, slender tree to 15 m, is noted for its attractive flowers, which remain in bloom over several weeks from July, and the brilliant colours of its autumn leaves. Chinese stewartia (*S. sinensis*) has a creamy white or pinkish bark.

Tupelo family *Nyssaceae*
Tupelo

Nyssa sylvatica

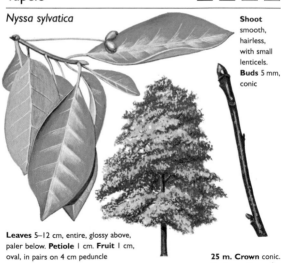

Shoot smooth, hairless, with small lenticels. **Buds** 5 mm, conic

Leaves 5–12 cm, entire, glossy above, paler below. **Petiole** 1 cm. **Fruit** 1 cm, oval, in pairs on 4 cm peduncle

25 m. Crown conic. **Bark** grey, fissured

The genus *Nyssa* comprises five species: three from eastern USA and two from China and SE Asia. Tupelo is the only common one, remaining a dull tree until early autumn when it becomes a blaze of glossy scarlet, gold, and finally red.

Davidia family *Davidiaceae*
Dove tree

R 🌳 🌿 🏛

Davidia involucrata

Flower
2 cm wide

20 m. Crown domed.
Bole short. **Branches**
radiate outwards. **Bark**
purplish, flaking brown,
with vertical fissures

Bracts large,
to 17 cm, in
uneven pairs,
paper-thin

Lenticels pale

Buds 1.5 cm,
conic, shiny

Leaves 15 cm, shiny above, softly hairy below.
Veins impressed. **Petiole** 15 cm. **Vilmoriniana leaf**
(below): 20 cm, coarsely serrate, glabrous below

Shoot
glabrous

Fruit 3 cm, hard, fleshy,
ribbed, ripening purple,
with prominent lenticels.
Pedicel 10 cm

Dedicated to its discoverer, Père Armand David, this is a vigorous,
lime-like tree native only to western China. Its appearance in May
can be very striking, when the large, white bracts which subtend
each flower drape the branches and give the tree its name.
D. involucrata var. *vilmoriniana* has larger leaves and is more
frequent than the type.

Myrtle family *Myrtaceae*
Cider gum

Eucalyptus gunnii

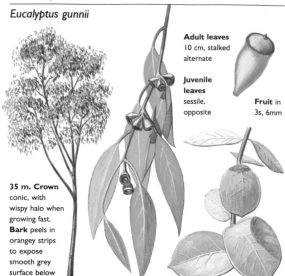

Adult leaves
10 cm, stalked
alternate

Juvenile leaves
sessile,
opposite

Fruit in
3s, 6mm

35 m. Crown
conic, with
wispy halo when
growing fast.
Bark peels in
orangey strips
to expose
smooth grey
surface below

Cider gum – so called as a cider can be made from the sap – is the hardiest gum. It is a native of Tasmania and coppices readily if cut back. The flowers before opening are covered by a cap (operculum) of fused petals.

Snow gum

Eucalpytus niphophila

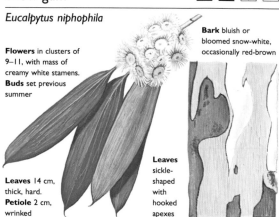

Flowers in clusters of
9–11, with mass of
creamy white stamens.
Buds set previous
summer

Bark bluish or
bloomed snow-white,
occasionally red-brown

Leaves
sickle-
shaped
with
hooked
apexes

Leaves 14 cm,
thick, hard.
Petiole 2 cm,
wrinked

A small tree reaching 10 m, Snow gum grows wild in south-eastern Australia at heights up to 2,000 m above sea-level. Blue gum (*E. globulus*), from Tasmania, has much larger leaves, glaucous blue when juvenile.

Ivy family *Araliaceae*
Ivy

Hedera helix

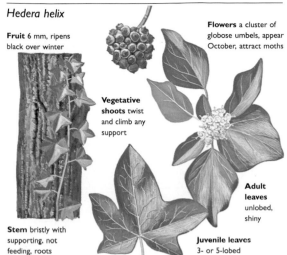

Fruit 6 mm, ripens black over winter

Flowers a cluster of globose umbels, appear October, attract moths

Vegetative shoots twist and climb any support

Adult leaves unlobed, shiny

Stem bristly with supporting, not feeding, roots

Juvenile leaves 3- or 5-lobed

Ivy is a plant which climbs to reach sunlight, but can easily be mistaken for a tree when its prolific growth and flowers blanket its host, which probably suffers no harm. It ceases climbing and flowers once the leaves are exposed to full light.

Prickly castor oil tree

Kalopanax septemlobus var. *maximowiczii*

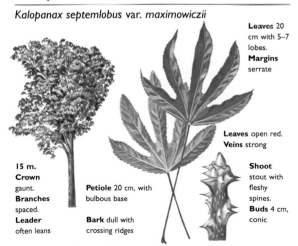

Leaves 20 cm with 5–7 lobes. **Margins** serrate

Leaves open red. **Veins** strong

15 m. Crown gaunt. **Branches** spaced. **Leader** often leans

Petiole 20 cm, with bulbous base

Bark dull with crossing ridges

Shoot stout with fleshy spines. **Buds** 4 cm, conic

Kalopanax is an unusual Asian genus comprising only one species. The variety shown here is the commonest but the type which has smaller leaves with shallower lobes is also occasionally seen. White flowers are carried in heads up to 60 cm across.

Dogwood family *Cornaceae*
Table dogwood

Cornus controversa

15 m. Branches in tiers. **Bark** grey, smooth, becoming cross-ridged. **Shoot** dark red, glabrous

Petiole 4 cm

Flowers each 1.5 cm, in upright cymes, June-July

Leaves hairy below

Leaves 12 cm, shiny, alternate; those of 'Variegata' narrower, creamy yellow and green, twisted

Table dogwood is a wide-ranging tree, extending from the Himalayas to Japan. Like all dogwoods it has leaves with basal veins curving parallel to the margin but, apart from one American species, *C. alternifolia*, is unique in its alternative leaves.

Nuttall dogwood

Cornus nuttallii

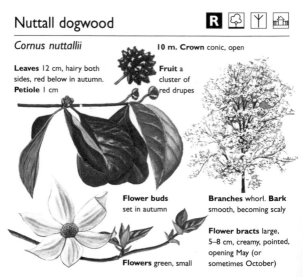

10 m. Crown conic, open

Leaves 12 cm, hairy both sides, red below in autumn. **Petiole** 1 cm

Fruit a cluster of red drupes

Flower buds set in autumn

Flowers green, small

Branches whorl. **Bark** smooth, becoming scaly

Flower bracts large, 5–8 cm, creamy, pointed, opening May (or sometimes October)

Presenting a magnificent display when the conspicuous bracts of its flower-heads open, Nuttall dogwood is a native of the North American west coast where it reaches 30 m. Flowering dogwood (*C. florida*) has smaller leaves and always has four bracts.

Japanese dogwood

Cornus kousa

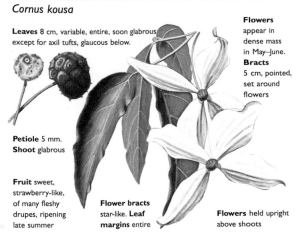

Leaves 8 cm, variable, entire, soon glabrous except for axil tufts, glaucous below.

Flowers appear in dense mass in May–June.
Bracts 5 cm, pointed, set around flowers

Petiole 5 mm.
Shoot glabrous

Fruit sweet, strawberry-like, of many fleshy drupes, ripening late summer

Flower bracts star-like. **Leaf margins** entire

Flowers held upright above shoots

This dogwood is native to Japan, Korea and central China and grows to 10 m. Its branches are somewhat tiered like those of Table dogwood, from which it can be distinguished by its opposite leaves. It is notable for its brilliant autumn reds.

Cornelian cherry

Cornus mas

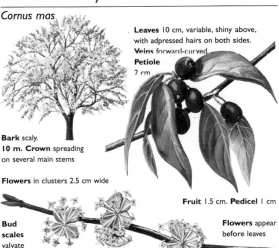

Leaves 10 cm, variable, shiny above, with adpressed hairs on both sides.
Veins forward-curved.
Petiole 2 cm

Bark scaly.
10 m. Crown spreading on several main stems

Flowers in clusters 2.5 cm wide

Fruit 1.5 cm. **Pedicel** 1 cm

Bud scales valvate

Flowers appear before leaves

Flowers 4 mm, with 4 bracts at cluster base

This ornamental is a native of southern Europe and has long been cultivated for the bright yellow flowers which cloak its bare branches in February and March and for its abundant fruit which provides another attractive display in October. This fruit is edible and can be made into jam or syrup.

Heather family *Ericaceae*
Strawberry tree

Arbutus unedo

Petiole
7 mm, hairy.
Shoot
long-haired

Leaves 10 cm,
variable, serrate, shiny,
very dark above, paler
below

Flowers
6 mm, pink
or white

Fruit 2 cm, warty, green-
yellow, ripening to orange-
pink as new flowers open

Panicles
of 15–20
flowers
open in
Oct–Dec

Native to south-west Ireland and southern Europe, the Strawberry
tree is a small evergreen up to 10 m high and has a dark red-
brown, finely fissured bark. Its strawberry-like fruit takes a year to
ripen. It can be eaten but its insipidness is indicated by the tree's
specific name *unedo* meaning "I eat (only) one."

Madroña

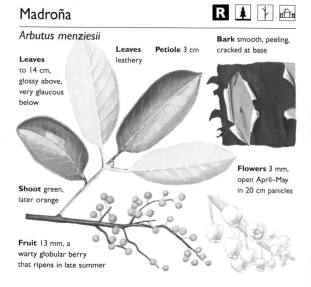

Arbutus menziesii

Leaves
to 14 cm,
glossy above,
very glaucous
below

Leaves
leathery

Petiole 3 cm

Bark smooth, peeling,
cracked at base

Shoot green,
later orange

Flowers 3 mm,
open April–May
in 20 cm panicles

Fruit 13 mm, a
warty globular berry
that ripens in late summer

Madroña is native to the Pacific of North America where it attains
40 m and is readily identified by its bark. Similar barks are carried
by the Greek strawberry tree (A. andrachne) which has narrower
leaves and A. x andrachnoides with serrate leaves.

Sorrel tree

Oxydendrum arboreum

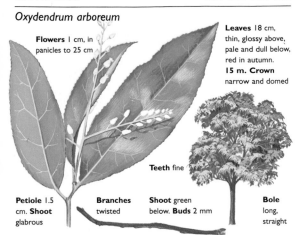

Flowers I cm, in panicles to 25 cm

Leaves 18 cm, thin, glossy above, pale and dull below, red in autumn. **15 m. Crown** narrow and domed

Teeth fine

Petiole 1.5 cm. **Shoot** glabrous

Branches twisted

Shoot green below. **Buds** 2 mm

Bole long, straight

Native to the eastern USA, Sorrel is unusual in flowering in autumn, its foliage often turning scarlet while it is still in flower. Its name refers to the pleasantly sour taste of its leaves. The fruit capsules are whitish and 12 mm wide.

Ebony family *Ebenaceae*

Persimmon

Diospyros virginiana

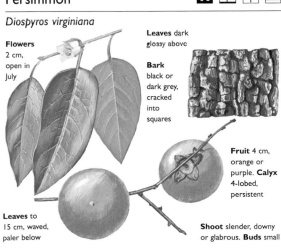

Flowers 2 cm, open in July

Leaves dark glossy above

Bark black or dark grey, cracked into squares

Fruit 4 cm, orange or purple. **Calyx** 4-lobed, persistent

Leaves to 15 cm, waved, paler below

Shoot slender, downy or glabrous. **Buds** small

Persimmon, from the south-eastern USA, grows up to 20 m and is distinguished by its glossy leaves, its hanging, urn-shaped flowers and its astringent fruit which is edible after exposure to autumn frosts. Date plum (*D. lotus*), an Asian relative, has petioles only 1 cm long and flowers 8 mm white.

Storax family *Styracaceae*
Snowbell tree

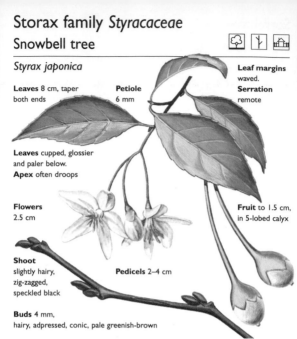

Styrax japonica

Leaves 8 cm, taper both ends

Petiole 6 mm

Leaf margins waved.
Serration remote

Leaves cupped, glossier and paler below.
Apex often droops

Flowers 2.5 cm

Fruit to 1.5 cm, in 5-lobed calyx

Shoot slightly hairy, zig-zagged, speckled black

Pedicels 2–4 cm

Buds 4 mm, hairy, adpressed, conic, pale greenish-brown

A native of Japan and China, the Snowbell tree grows to 10 m with a dense, rounded crown of horizontal branches. Storax (*S. officinalis*) is a smaller tree with white down on the young twigs, leaves and flowers. It has ovate, cordate leaves and round fruits.

Bigleaf storax

Styrax obassia

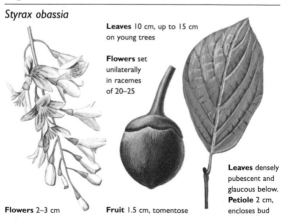

Leaves 10 cm, up to 15 cm on young trees

Flowers set unilaterally in racemes of 20–25

Leaves densely pubescent and glaucous below.
Petiole 2 cm, encloses bud

Flowers 2–3 cm

Fruit 1.5 cm, tomentose

Native to Japan, Bigleaf storax has a grey bark and an open, upright crown that reaches 15 m. Hemsley storax (*S. hemsleyana*) carries its white flowers on short, pubescent racemes. The petioles of its less downy leaves do not enclose the bud.

Snowdrop tree

Halesia monticola

Leaves finely serrate

Leaves 15 cm, hairy below.
Leaf stalk 1 cm, grooved, pubescent.
Shoot hairy at first, soon glabrous

Veins impressed

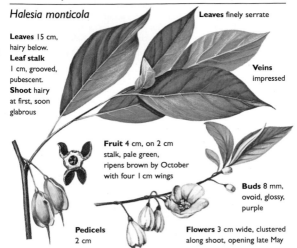

Fruit 4 cm, on 2 cm stalk, pale green, ripens brown by October with four 1 cm wings

Buds 8 mm, ovoid, glossy, purple

Pedicels 2 cm

Flowers 3 cm wide, clustered along shoot, opening late May

Snowdrop tree is native to the mountains of the south-eastern USA and is distinguished by its fruit and flowers. Carolina snowdrop (*H. carolina*) is shrubbier with smaller flowers and fruit.

Loosestrife family *Lythraceae*

Crape myrtle

Lagerstroemia indica

Flowers terminate new shoots.
Petals (6) crinkled, on long peduncle

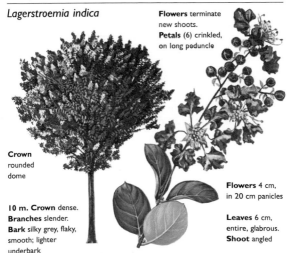

Crown rounded dome

10 m. Crown dense.
Branches slender.
Bark silky grey, flaky, smooth; lighter underbark

Flowers 4 cm, in 20 cm panicles

Leaves 6 cm, entire, glabrous.
Shoot angled

This native of China and Japan only produces its splendid flowers in climates with long, hot summers. The flowers are usually bright pink but can be white, purple or scarlet. The buds and leaves may be set in pairs, threes or singly along the same shoot.

Olive family *Oleaceae*

The main features of this family of about 400 trees and shrubs are the opposite, simple or pinnate leaves and the perfect or unisexual flowers with 2 stamens. The fruit may be a drupe, capsule or samara. Ash is the main tree genus and has fissured barks and shoots flattened between the buds. The fruit is a samara while *Olea*, *Ligustrum* and *Phillyrea* have simple leaves and a drupaceous fruit.

Ash

Fraxinus excelsior

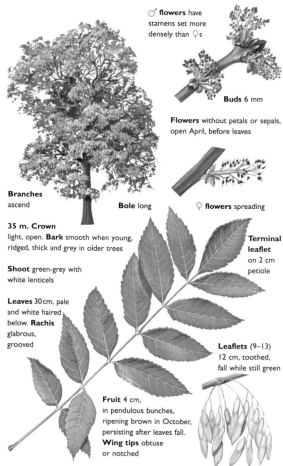

♂ **flowers** have stamens set more densely than ♀s

Buds 6 mm

Flowers without petals or sepals, open April, before leaves

Branches ascend

Bole long

♀ **flowers** spreading

35 m. Crown light, open. **Bark** smooth when young, ridged, thick and grey in older trees

Terminal leaflet on 2 cm petiole

Shoot green-grey with white lenticels

Leaves 30 cm, pale and white haired below. **Rachis** glabrous, grooved

Leaflets (9–13) 12 cm, toothed, fall while still green

Fruit 4 cm, in pendulous bunches, ripening brown in October, persisting after leaves fall. **Wing tips** obtuse or notched

Native throughout Europe and Asia Minor, Ash is a large forest tree that grows best on heavy, alkaline loams. While male and female flowers normally appear on separate trees, one tree may carry both sexes. The squat, black buds and smooth twigs are its best identification features. Red ash (*F. pennsylvanica*) has reddish buds, 7–9 leaflets and a brown, shallowly fissured bark.

Some cultivars of Ash

'Pendula': 10 m. Crown grafted at height of 3 m (or higher) to rootstock of Ash. **Branches** twist

'Jaspidea': Shoot yellow or golden by end of summer, flattened near bud. **Bud** 6 mm, black, true to type

Leaflet (above) yellow in spring, gold in autumn

'Diversifolia': Leaves (right) simple, occasionally trifoliate. **Petiole** 10 cm. **Veins** prominent below. **Bud** black

Serration very variable, usually coarse but sometimes very fine

'Pendula' or Weeping ash is readily identified by its habit, although one form reaching 30 m is less weeping and has some erect shoots. 'Jaspidea' is noted for its yellow shoots and foliage. The leaves and crown of 'Diversifolia' can confuse identification but the fruit, twigs and buds are identical to the type.

Manna ash

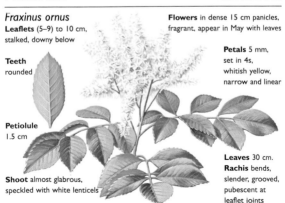

Fraxinus ornus
Leaflets (5–9) to 10 cm, stalked, downy below

Flowers in dense 15 cm panicles, fragrant, appear in May with leaves

Teeth rounded

Petals 5 mm, set in 4s, whitish yellow, narrow and linear

Petiolule 1.5 cm

Leaves 30 cm. **Rachis** bends, slender, grooved, pubescent at leaflet joints

Shoot almost glabrous, speckled with white lenticels

Manna ash reaches 20 m to form a tree similar to *F. excelsior*, but distinguished from it, when not in flower, by its stalked, pubescent leaflets and grey-brown, hairy buds. It grows wild in southern Europe and western Asia and is sometimes tapped for the sugary substance which exudes from the bark and gives the tree its common name.

Caucasian ash

Fraxinus oxycarpa

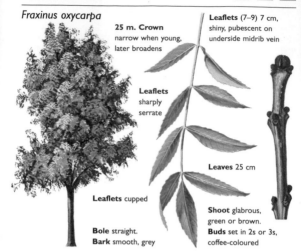

25 m. Crown narrow when young, later broadens

Leaflets (7–9) 7 cm, shiny, pubescent on underside midrib vein

Leaflets sharply serrate

Leaves 25 cm

Leaflets cupped

Bole straight.
Bark smooth, grey

Shoot glabrous, green or brown.
Buds set in 2s or 3s, coffee-coloured

This ash grows wild from southern Europe across the Caucasus to Iran and is usually encountered as the clone 'Raywood', whose leaves turn claret in autumn. Narrow-leafed ash (*F. angustifolia*) has slender, glabrous leaflets and a rougher, dark grey bark.

Velvet ash

R

Fraxinus velutina

Buds 5 mm, velvety, 6-scaled

Fruit 2 cm on downy pedicel. **Wing** shorter than seed, notched

Leaflets downy

Shoot round, slender, velvety in 1st year

Leaflets 5 cm, thick, bluntly toothed above middle, usually in 5s or, less often, 3s, 7s and 9s

Leaf 15 cm

Although some forms are almost glabrous, Velvet or Arizona ash, from the south-western USA and Mexico, has pubescence even on its flower panicles. It can stand great extremes of temperature and reaches 10 or 15 m. The bark is broadly ridged.

Olive

Olea europaea

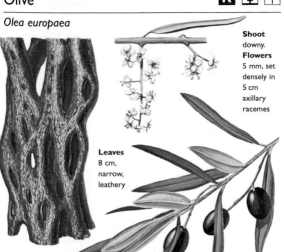

Shoot downy.
Flowers 5 mm, set densely in 5 cm axillary racemes

Leaves 8 cm, narrow, leathery

Bole gnarled, dimpled

Bark ridged, plated in small squares

Fruit a 3 cm drupe

A common feature of the Mediterranean landscape, the Olive has a densely branched crown that reaches 15 m as an orchard tree but when growing wild is much shrubbier and has small, oval leaves. If to be eaten, the fruit is usually harvested when green; for oil production it is generally left until black and fully ripe.

Chinese or Tree privet

Ligustrum lucidum

Leaves 10 cm, entire, folded along midrib, dark, glossy above, paler and matt below

Flowers creamy-white, fragrant, in many 15 cm conic panicles in Aug–Sept

15 m. Crown dense

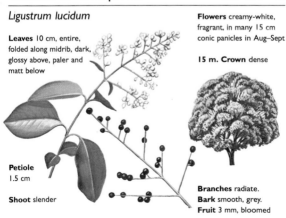

Petiole 1.5 cm

Shoot slender

Branches radiate.
Bark smooth, grey.
Fruit 3 mm, bloomed

This superb Chinese evergreen is noted for its glossy and leathery leaves and the lateness of its flowers which open in autumn. Lilac (*Syringa vulgaris*) flowers in May and June and is deciduous with stout shoots ending in large pairs of green buds.

Phillyrea

Phillyrea latifolia

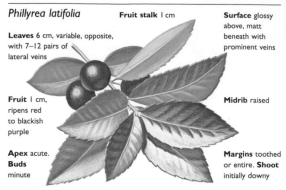

Fruit stalk 1 cm

Surface glossy above, matt beneath with prominent veins

Leaves 6 cm, variable, opposite, with 7–12 pairs of lateral veins

Fruit 1 cm, ripens red to blackish purple

Midrib raised

Apex acute. **Buds** minute

Margins toothed or entire. **Shoot** initially downy

Phillyrea, found in evergreen woods in the Mediterranean region, reaches 10 m. It has a rounded crown with very glossy foliage which appears almost black, and a dense, shrub-like habit. The bark is smooth and grey. Its small, whitish green flowers appear in short axillary clusters during June.

Figwort family *Scrophulariaceae*

Paulownia

Paulownia tomentosa

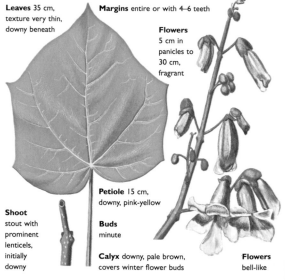

Leaves 35 cm, texture very thin, downy beneath

Margins entire or with 4–6 teeth

Flowers 5 cm in panicles to 30 cm, fragrant

Petiole 15 cm, downy, pink-yellow

Shoot stout with prominent lenticels, initially downy

Buds minute

Calyx downy, pale brown, covers winter flower buds

Flowers bell-like

A native of China, Paulownia, also called Foxglove tree, has a gaunt, domed crown and reaches 20 m. The flowers are often damaged over winter when fully exposed in bud. They are followed by green, ovoid, pointed capsules containing winged seeds.

Bignonia family *Bignoniaceae*

Indian bean tree • Northern catalpa

Catalpa bignonioides • Catalpa speciosa

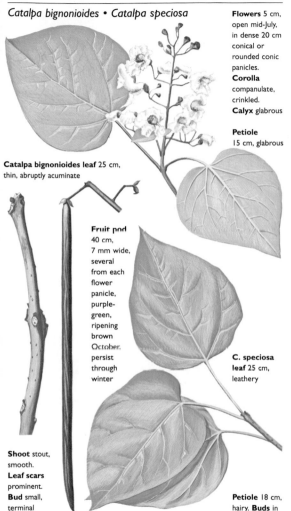

Flowers 5 cm, open mid-July, in dense 20 cm conical or rounded conic panicles. **Corolla** companulate, crinkled. **Calyx** glabrous

Petiole 15 cm, glabrous

Catalpa bignonioides leaf 25 cm, thin, abruptly acuminate

Fruit pod 40 cm, 7 mm wide, several from each flower panicle, purple-green, ripening brown October, persist through winter

C. speciosa leaf 25 cm, leathery

Shoot stout, smooth. **Leaf scars** prominent. **Bud** small, terminal lacking

Petiole 18 cm, hairy. **Buds** in 2s or 3s

The catalpas are a small group of trees with large ovate leaves and long, hanging pods. The commonest, Indian bean tree, from the gulf coast of America, forms a low, spreading tree, occasionally to 20 m. Northern catalpa, from central USA, has a conic crown and may attain 40 m, or half this height in Europe. Its flowers, to 6 cm, open earlier and the calyx is hairy. Chinese Yellow catalpa (*C. ovata*) has yellower 3 cm flowers and broadly ovate 3-lobed leaves with long tips. Hybrid catalpa (*C. x erubescens*) has leaves opening purple. Farges catalpa (*C. fargesii*) has pink flowers.

Agave family *Agavaceae*
Cabbage palm

Cordyline australis

Leaves 90 cm, lanceolate, pointed tip, erect, later drooping, persisting dead

10 m

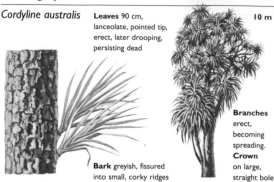

Branches erect, becoming spreading.
Crown on large, straight bole

Bark greyish, fissured into small, corky ridges

Cabbage palm, from New Zealand, is hardy in coastal regions. Leaves are arranged spirally in tufts on shoots. The fragrant, creamy-white flowers are carried in terminal panicles up to 1 m high and are followed by numerous 6 mm bluish-white berries.

Palm family *Palmaceae*
Chusan palm

Trachycarpus fortunei

Bark in cloth-like layers; peels in sheets

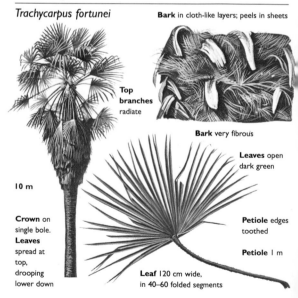

Top branches radiate

Bark very fibrous

Leaves open dark green

10 m

Crown on single bole.
Leaves spread at top, drooping lower down

Petiole edges toothed

Petiole 1 m

Leaf 120 cm wide, in 40–60 folded segments

Chusan palm, also called Windmill palm, from central China, is the palm most tolerant of cold and remarkable for its cloth-like bark. Like all true palms it has only a single growing point and so never branches.

Index

Entries refer to subspecies, varieties and cultivars described in detail and illustrated – for related trees, see genus or nearest species entry.